Jeremy Flint is a World Life Master of the World Bridge Federation, Grand Master of the English Bridge Union and Life Master of the American Contract Bridge League. He has competed in numerous international bridge tournaments and is the author of six previous books on bridge. He is the bridge correspondent of *The Times* and has appeared, both as player and as commentator, in the television series *Grand Slam* and *Bridge Club*, a series for beginners.

Freddie North has won most of the major competitions in his own country and is one of Great Britain's most successful rubber bridge players. He represented Britain at the 1960 and 1964 World Pairs Olympiads and has played in many international matches. He is a bridge and racing journalist. Principal of the Sussex School of Bridge, he lives in Hove, Sussex.

Also by Jeremy Flint and Freddie North
in Sphere Books:

BRIDGE: THE GOLDEN PRINCIPLES

Jeremy Flint and
Freddie North

Bridge:
the first principles

SPHERE BOOKS LIMITED

A Sphere Book

First published in Great Britain by Pan Books Ltd 1985
(Dummy section first published as a card pack 1979)
Published by Sphere Books 1989

Printed and bound in Great Britain by
Cox & Wyman Ltd, Reading

Sphere Books Ltd
A Division of
Macdonald & Co. (Publishers) Ltd.
27 Wrights Lane, London W8 5TZ
A member of Maxwell Pergamon Publishing Corporation plc

Introduction

Bridge is the most paradoxical of games. As with the English language, the exceptions sometimes seem to outnumber the rules. We believe that this tantalizing aspect is to some degree responsible for the game's spell-binding fascination.

The comparison with English is only partially valid. Whereas we cannot see any reason why 'rough' and 'plough' should be pronounced differently, the exceptions at bridge have a logical explanation. The contradictions are only superficial.

Our objective in this book is two-fold: to illustrate the fundamental technique of card play and the occasions when you should break the 'rules'; and to increase the value of the examples by attaching a principle which extends to innumerable other hands of the same type. So on every right-hand page of this book you will find an example of a hand which poses a question. On the next page you will find the answer to that question, plus an explanation of the principle involved.

To explain a theme fully we sometimes present three hands of a similar nature. By design, these hands have not been placed in groups, as you might find in a standard textbook. We have deliberately separated them so that you can check your progress. Obviously we hope that when you see a theme for the second time you will recognize the point. When you do, it is a sure sign of improvement.

Everyone agrees that defence is difficult. So do not become discouraged if you fail to find the solution initially. If you absorb the principle we advocate, you will achieve a sound grasp of the subject.

Flair may be a desirable quality for a card player, but in our experience it is a poor substitute for study and perseverance.

Dummy play

When you first learn bridge, playing the dummy seems a big responsibility. There are many pitfalls. So many things to remember. So much to think about all at the same time.

Our experience has taught us the sort of hands which beginners find difficult. If you study these examples and master the principle involved, you will have taken a giant stride on the path to becoming a competent dummy player.

Contents

Card combinations

With no special guide from the bidding, how would you play these card combinations? (The answers are on the reverse.

1	A Q J 10 x x x x x x	With up to ten cards, missing the king. $\begin{smallmatrix}&N&\\W&&E\\&S&\end{smallmatrix}$

2	A Q J 10 x x x x x x x	With eleven cards, missing the king. $\begin{smallmatrix}&N&\\W&&E\\&S&\end{smallmatrix}$

3	A K J 10 x x x x	With eight cards, missing the queen. $\begin{smallmatrix}&N&\\W&&E\\&S&\end{smallmatrix}$

4	A K J 10 x x x x x	With nine cards, missing the queen. $\begin{smallmatrix}&N&\\W&&E\\&S&\end{smallmatrix}$

5	A K J 10 x x x x	With eight cards (6 opposite 2), missing the queen. $\begin{smallmatrix}&N&\\W&&E\\&S&\end{smallmatrix}$

6	A J 10 9 x x x x x	With up to nine cards, missing the king and queen. $\begin{smallmatrix}&N&\\W&&E\\&S&\end{smallmatrix}$

7	K Q 9 x x J 8 x x	With nine cards, missing the ace and ten. $\begin{smallmatrix}&N&\\W&&E\\&S&\end{smallmatrix}$

8	K Q 9 x x J 8 x	With eight cards, missing the ace and ten. $\begin{smallmatrix}&N&\\W&&E\\&S&\end{smallmatrix}$

9	K 8 x x x x Q 10 x x	With ten cards, missing the ace and knave. $\begin{smallmatrix}&N&\\W&&E\\&S&\end{smallmatrix}$

10	A 10 9 x x K x	With seven cards, missing the queen and knave. $\begin{smallmatrix}&N&\\W&&E\\&S&\end{smallmatrix}$

Card combinations – answers

1 A Q J 10 x   Finesse the queen, hoping that West has the
   x x x x x   king.

2 A Q J 10 x x Play the ace, hoping that the king will drop.
   x x x x x

3 A K J 10 x   Play the ace first and then finesse the
   x x x
                 knave on the next round, hoping that West
                 has the queen.

4 A K J 10 x   Play the ace and king, hoping that the queen
   x x x x   will drop.

5 A K J 10 x x Take a first round finesse, catering for four to
   x x   the queen with West.

6 A J 10 9 x   Finesse the knave and then the ten.
   x x x x

7 K Q 9 x x   Lead small to the king, restricting your
   J 8 x x
                 loss to one trick with any distribution.

8 K Q 9 x x   Lead small to the king, and then to the
   J 8 x
                 knave. This caters for A 10 x x or a singleton
                 ace with West.

9 K 8 x x x x   Lead small to the king, or play the
   Q 10 x x
                 king. This fails only if East is void.

10 A 10 9 x x   Play the king and then (unless East
   K x
                 shows out) the ace. Continue with the
                 ten. This line restricts the losers to one
                 whenever the suit is divided 3–3, or when
                 there is a doubleton honour in either hand.

1. E-W game; dealer South. Contract: 4S by South.

$\spadesuit$ J 10 9 4
$\heartsuit$ 6 4 3 2
$\diamondsuit$ A 5
$\clubsuit$ K Q 8

$\spadesuit$ A K Q 8 7 5
$\heartsuit$ 10 8
$\diamondsuit$ 7 4
$\clubsuit$ A 9 6

The bidding

S	W	N	E
1$\spadesuit$	2$\heartsuit$	3$\spadesuit$	Pass
4$\spadesuit$	Pass	Pass	Pass

West leads the ace, king and queen of hearts. How should South plan the play?

Making a lay-down contract

1. E-W game: dealer South.   Contract: 4S by South.

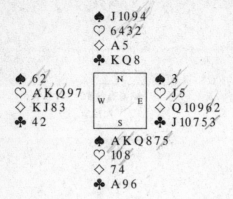

```
                    ♠ J 10 9 4
                    ♡ 6 4 3 2
                    ◇ A 5
                    ♣ K Q 8
    ♠ 6 2              N           ♠ 3
    ♡ A K Q 9 7                    ♡ J 5
    ◇ K J 8 3      W       E       ◇ Q 10 9 6 2
    ♣ 4 2              S           ♣ J 10 7 5 3
                    ♠ A K Q 8 7 5
                    ♡ 10 8
                    ◇ 7 4
                    ♣ A 9 6
```

The play

South has a simple task. He ruffs the third round of hearts, draws the opponents' trumps and cashes his winners. He makes: 6 spades, 1 diamond and 3 clubs.

The principle

On this occasion the hand is lay-down. Nevertheless declarer would be wise to follow the routine that should precede the play of every hand. *Count the sure tricks*. If they are insufficient, *look for ways of establishing the additional winners that are required. Consider the snags and difficulties. Above all, make a plan (remember that the bidding and opening lead are often significant)*. On this hand the sure tricks total ten. There is no need to establish extra tricks. There are no snags. This is the straightforward plan: ruff the third round of hearts, draw the opponents' trumps and cash the winners.

Note that it would be entirely futile to ruff dummy's last heart, though many beginners would do so. South can make exactly six spade tricks, whether he ruffs or not.

2. N-S game; dealer South.   Contract: 4H by South.

♠ 8
♡ J 10 3
♢ 6 5 4 3 2
♣ A 7 4 2

♠ A J 7
♡ A K Q 9 6
♢ Q 7
♣ K 6 3

The bidding

S	W	N	E
1♡	2♢	2♡	Pass
4♡	Pass	Pass	Pass

West leads the ace, king and knave of diamonds. East throws small spades on the second and third rounds of diamonds. How should South plan the play?

Ruffing in dummy before drawing trumps

2. N-S game; dealer South.   Contract: 4H by South.

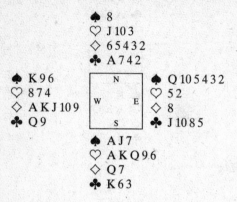

```
                    ♠ 8
                    ♡ J 10 3
                    ◇ 6 5 4 3 2
                    ♣ A 7 4 2
   ♠ K 9 6                          ♠ Q 10 5 4 3 2
   ♡ 8 7 4              N           ♡ 5 2
   ◇ A K J 10 9    W       E        ◇ 8
   ♣ Q 9                            ♣ J 10 8 5
                        S
                    ♠ A J 7
                    ♡ A K Q 9 6
                    ◇ Q 7
                    ♣ K 6 3
```

The play

South should ruff the third round of diamonds and continue with
the ace and another spade, ruffing with dummy's ♡10. He
should return to his hand with the ♣K and ruff a second spade
with dummy's ♡J. Now he can draw trumps and cash the ♣A,
making ten tricks: 5 hearts, 1 spade, 2 spade ruffs and 2 clubs.

The principle

Although it is usual to draw trumps as early as possible, in order
to prevent the opposition ruffing your winners, there are many
occasions when this task has to be postponed. In this instance
declarer discovers that his total number of winners is only eight
(♠A, ♣AK and five trump tricks). Therefore he must plan to
develop the two extra tricks by taking two spade ruffs in the
short trump hand (dummy is usually, but not always, the short
trump hand).

   Note that a ruff in the *short* trump hand is always pure profit –
on this occasion, South makes seven trump tricks instead of five.

3. Love all; dealer North.   Contract: 4S by South.

♠ A 5 3
♡ K 5 2
♢ A 4 2
♣ A 10 9 7

♠ K Q J 10 8
♡ A 9 6 3
♢ 7 5 3
♣ 2

The bidding

N	S
1♣	1♠
1 NT	3♡
3♠	4♠

West leads the queen of diamonds. How should South plan the play?

3. Love all; dealer North.   Contract: 4S by South.

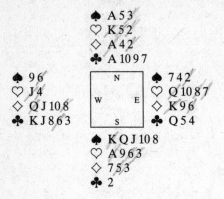

```
              ♠ A 5 3
              ♡ K 5 2
              ◇ A 4 2
              ♣ A 10 9 7
  ♠ 9 6          N          ♠ 7 4 2
  ♡ J 4                     ♡ Q 10 8 7
  ◇ Q J 10 8  W     E       ◇ K 9 6
  ♣ K J 8 6 3     S         ♣ Q 5 4
              ♠ K Q J 10 8
              ♡ A 9 6 3
              ◇ 7 5 3
              ♣ 2
```

The play
South should win with the ◇A, cash *one* top trump only (♠K) and then play the ace, king and another heart. The defence may play a second trump, but nothing can stop declarer obtaining a heart ruff in dummy with the ace of trumps. Declarer makes: 5 spades, 2 hearts, 1 heart ruff in dummy and one trick in each of the minors.

The principle
When there are losers in his own hand, declarer should consider whether ruffs can be taken in dummy before drawing trumps. In this instance declarer has nine top tricks, so his aim is to gain a heart ruff in dummy if the suit fails to divide 3–3. It is correct to cash the ace and king of hearts and exit with a third heart, so that the defenders are unable to ruff one of the masters. Notice that it is unsafe to draw more than one round of trumps, because (assuming two rounds are taken) the defender winning the third round of hearts could play a third trump, preventing a ruff in dummy.

4. E-W game; dealer South.   Contract: 2D by South.

♠ 7 4 2
♥ 10 5 3
♦ K 9 4
♣ A Q 7 2

♠ A 8 6
♥ Q 7 2
♦ A Q J 10 6
♣ 8 4

The bidding

S	W	N	E
1♦	1♥	2♦	Pass
Pass	Pass		

West leads the six of hearts to East's ace. West then takes two more heart tricks, East discarding a small spade at trick three, and switches to a trump. How should South plan the play?

Taking a finesse

4. E-W game; dealer South.   Contract: 2D by South.

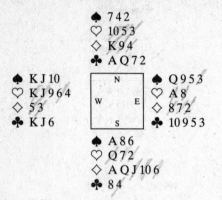

```
              ♠ 7 4 2
              ♡ 10 5 3
              ◇ K 9 4
              ♣ A Q 7 2
  ♠ K J 10                    ♠ Q 9 5 3
  ♡ K J 9 6 4        N        ♡ A 8
  ◇ 5 3         W       E     ◇ 8 7 2
  ♣ K J 6           S         ♣ 10 9 5 3
              ♠ A 8 6
              ♡ Q 7 2
              ◇ A Q J 10 6
              ♣ 8 4
```

The play
South should draw trumps and take the club 'finesse' – that is, he should play a club towards the AQ and, when West follows with the six, play the queen. With the ♣K favourably placed the finesse succeeds. South makes: 5 diamonds, 1 spade and 2 clubs.

The principle
When you finesse you hope to take advantage of a particular card being well placed. In this example the ♣K lies under the AQ, so you make two club tricks. If East had had the ♣K you could have made only one club trick and the contract would have been defeated. It is important to appreciate that South did not *know* that the ♣Q would win – he hoped it would, and it did.

5. Love all; dealer South.   Contract: 3 NT by South.

                              ♠ K 8 6 4
                              ♡ J 6
                              ◇ A J 10
                              ♣ Q 6 5 3

                          ┌─────────────┐
                          │   N   │
                          │ W   E │
                          │   S   │
                          └─────────────┘

                              ♠ A 5 3
                              ♡ A 8 4
                              ◇ 9 7 5
                              ♣ A K J 10

The bidding

          S   N
          1♣   1♠
          1 NT   3 NT

West leads the three of hearts. South tries the ♡J from dummy,
but when East plays the queen South correctly refuses to win his
ace until forced to do so on the third round. How should South
plan the play?

The double finesse

5. Love all; dealer South. Contract: 3 NT by South.

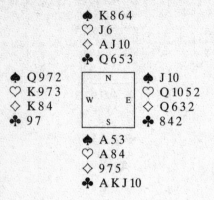

```
              ♠ K 8 6 4
              ♡ J 6
              ◇ A J 10
              ♣ Q 6 5 3
♠ Q 9 7 2        N        ♠ J 10
♡ K 9 7 3                 ♡ Q 10 5 2
◇ K 8 4      W     E      ◇ Q 6 3 2
♣ 9 7            S        ♣ 8 4 2
              ♠ A 5 3
              ♡ A 8 4
              ◇ 9 7 5
              ♣ A K J 10
```

The play
South should continue with a small diamond towards dummy, inserting the 10 when West plays low. Although he loses this trick to the ◇Q he traps the ◇K under the AJ by repeating the finesse. South makes: 4 clubs, 2 spades, 2 diamonds and 1 heart.

The principle
When there are *two* vital outstanding honours (in this case the ◇KQ) you must finesse twice. Begin by playing a diamond towards dummy's ◇AJ10. If this loses, return to hand and repeat the finesse. To find one card right is only even money, but it is 3–1 on finding at least one of the two missing honours correctly placed.

6. Game all; dealer South.　　　　Contract: 4S by South.

♠ K 8 6
♡ 10 8 6
♢ K 9 8 7 2
♣ 5 4

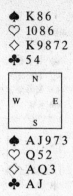

♠ A J 9 7 3
♡ Q 5 2
♢ A Q 3
♣ A J

The bidding

S	N
1♠	2♠
3♢	4♢
4♠	

West leads the four of hearts to East's ace. East returns the nine of hearts to West's knave. West now cashes the king of hearts, East throwing the seven of clubs, and switches to the two of clubs. East plays the queen of clubs at trick four, so South has to win with the ace. How should declarer play the trump suit, and in which order should he play the top diamonds?

6. Game all; dealer South.   Contract: 4S by South.

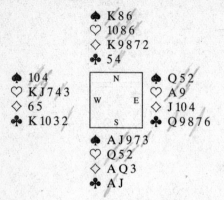

♠ K 8 6
♡ 10 8 6
♢ K 9 8 7 2
♣ 5 4

♠ 10 4
♡ K J 7 4 3
♢ 6 5
♣ K 10 3 2

♠ Q 5 2
♡ A 9
♢ J 10 4
♣ Q 9 8 7 6

♠ A J 9 7 3
♡ Q 5 2
♢ A Q 3
♣ A J

The play

Having already lost the three tricks he can afford, South must bring in the spade suit without loss, so he plays low to the king and finesses the knave on the way back. When the knave holds and everyone follows, he draws the remaining trump with the ♠A. Declarer must be careful to play the diamond honours in the correct order – the ace and queen first and then the three to the king. Declarer makes: 5 spades, 4 diamonds and 1 club.

The principle

When you cannot afford to lose a trick in an eight-card suit, missing the queen, the correct play is to finesse for the queen. In the above hand, the position of the knave means that you must finesse through East. Also, you should always take care to avoid blocking your suits. If, for example, you were to play the ♢A followed by the ♢3 to the king, you would be stranded in your own hand after winning the queen, and you would no longer be able to enjoy the club discard.

7. Game all; dealer South.   Contract: 3 NT by South.

> ♠ J863
> ♡ AK52
> ◇ 74
> ♣ 1053

```
        N
  W           E
        S
```

> ♠ AK5
> ♡ 96
> ◇ A93
> ♣ KQJ94

The bidding

S	N
1♣	1♡
2 NT	3 NT

West leads the king of diamonds. How should South plan the play?

Severing communications

7. Game all; dealer South.   Contract: 3 NT by South.

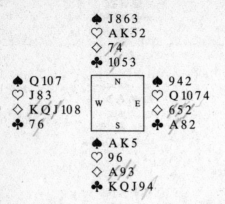

```
                    ♠ J863
                    ♡ AK52
                    ◇ 74
                    ♣ 1053
     ♠ Q107        ┌─────────┐      ♠ 942
     ♡ J83         │    N    │      ♡ Q1074
     ◇ KQJ108      │ W     E │      ◇ 652
     ♣ 76          │    S    │      ♣ A82
                   └─────────┘
                    ♠ AK5
                    ♡ 96
                    ◇ A93
                    ♣ KQJ94
```

The play
Declarer should withhold the ◇A until the third round. He should then knock out the ♣A. Fortunately, East holds this card and cannot put his partner in to cash the winning diamonds, so declarer makes: 4 clubs, 2 hearts, 2 spades and 1 diamond.

The principle
When the opponents lead your one danger suit in a no-trump contract, you may be able to sever their communications by withholding your card of control. Should the diamonds be divided 4–4 in the above hand, nothing will be lost by your precaution, and if the hand with the long diamonds has the vital ♣A you are doomed anyway.

8. Game all; dealer North.   Contract: 4S by South.

♠ A 5 3
♡ 8
♢ 8 7 6 3
♣ A K J 6 3

♠ K Q J 10 9
♡ A K 6
♢ 5 4 2
♣ 4 2

The bidding

S	W	N	E
—	—	1♣	Pass
1♠	Double	2♣	Pass
4♠	Pass	Pass	Pass

West leads the four top diamonds, East following to the first round and then discarding three small hearts. How should South plan the play?

When to ruff high

8. Game all; dealer North.   Contract: 4S by South.

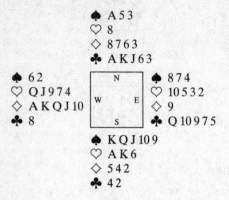

```
              ♠ A 5 3
              ♡ 8
              ◇ 8 7 6 3
              ♣ A K J 6 3
  ♠ 6 2            N         ♠ 8 7 4
  ♡ Q J 9 7 4                ♡ 10 5 3 2
  ◇ A K Q J 10   W     E     ◇ 9
  ♣ 8              S         ♣ Q 10 9 7 5
              ♠ K Q J 10 9
              ♡ A K 6
              ◇ 5 4 2
              ♣ 4 2
```

The play
South should ruff the fourth diamond, cash the ♡A and then ruff the ♡6 with the ♠A. He can now draw trumps and claim the rest of the tricks. Declarer makes: 5 spades, 2 hearts, 1 heart ruff and 2 clubs.

The principle
'Don't send a boy to do a man's job!' When you can afford to ruff high make sure you do so and avoid the risk of being overruffed.

9. Game all; dealer South.   Contract: 3 NT by South.

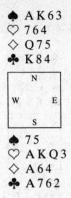

♠ A K 6 3
♡ 7 6 4
♢ Q 7 5
♣ K 8 4

♠ 7 5
♡ A K Q 3
♢ A 6 4
♣ A 7 6 2

The bidding

S	N
1♣	1♠
2 NT	3 NT

West leads the queen of clubs. How should South plan the play?

The finesse that is

9. Game all; dealer South.   Contract: 3 NT by South.

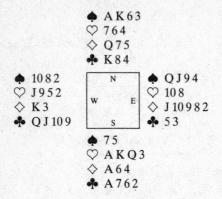

```
                    ♠ A K 6 3
                    ♡ 7 6 4
                    ◇ Q 7 5
                    ♣ K 8 4
  ♠ 10 8 2        ┌─────────┐      ♠ Q J 9 4
  ♡ J 9 5 2       │    N    │      ♡ 10 8
  ◇ K 3           │ W     E │      ◇ J 10 9 8 2
  ♣ Q J 10 9      │    S    │      ♣ 5 3
                  └─────────┘
                    ♠ 7 5
                    ♡ A K Q 3
                    ◇ A 6 4
                    ♣ A 7 6 2
```

The play

South should duck the first club and win the continuation in his own hand. He now plays a low diamond *towards* dummy's queen. Thus he makes the contract with: 2 spades, 3 hearts, 2 diamonds and 2 clubs. Note that the heart break is an extra chance for declarer that will not run away.

The principle

It is not a finesse to play an unsupported queen towards the ace, although you often see inexperienced players do it. In fact, against competent defence, it is a play guaranteed to lose no matter how the suit is divided. But to play the ace and another (or a small one without cashing the ace when, as here, it is necessary to retain control) towards the queen is by definition a normal finesse. You hope that the king will be placed in front of the queen.

10. E-W game; dealer South.   Contract: 4H by South.

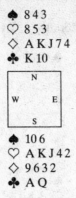

♠ 843
♡ 853
◇ A K J 74
♣ K 10

♠ 106
♡ A K J 42
◇ 9632
♣ A Q

The bidding

S	W	N	E
1♡	1♠	2◇	Pass
3◇	Pass	3♡	Pass
4♡	Pass	Pass	Pass

West leads the ace, king and queen of spades, East following with the two, five and knave. How should South plan the play?

Finesse or drop?

10. E-W game; dealer South.   Contract: 4H by South.

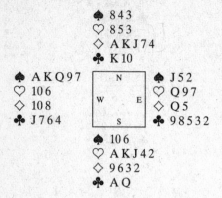

```
              ♠ 843
              ♡ 853
              ◇ AKJ74
              ♣ K10
  ♠ AKQ97    ┌─────────┐    ♠ J52
  ♡ 106      │    N    │    ♡ Q97
  ◇ 108      │ W     E │    ◇ Q5
  ♣ J764     │    S    │    ♣ 98532
              └─────────┘
              ♠ 106
              ♡ AKJ42
              ◇ 9632
              ♣ AQ
```

The play
Declarer should ruff the third spade and cash the ♡A. He now
leads the ♣Q to dummy's king and returns a heart towards the
closed hand, finessing the knave. Declarer draws the last trump
with the ♡K and then, when everyone follows to the ◇A, he
cashes the ◇K and, when the ◇Q drops, claims the remainder
of the tricks. He makes: 5 hearts, 4 diamonds and 2 clubs.

The principle
Normally it is correct to finesse when holding eight cards missing
the queen. The most probable break is 3–2, and the queen is
more likely to be with the trebleton than the doubleton. With
nine cards missing the queen and with no clues from the bidding
or early play, it is usually correct to rely on the drop.

11. Game all; dealer South.   Contract: 3 NT by South.

♠ K Q 6 4
♡ Q 2
♢ 10 8 5 2
♣ K J 9

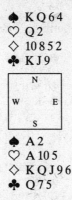

♠ A 2
♡ A 10 5
♢ K Q J 9 6
♣ Q 7 5

The bidding

S	N
1♢	1♠
1 NT	3 NT

West leads the six of hearts. How should South plan the play?

11. Game all; dealer South.   Contract: 3 NT by South.

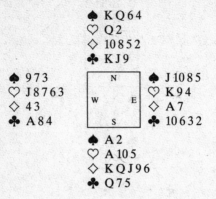

```
               ♠ K Q 6 4
               ♡ Q 2
               ◇ 10 8 5 2
               ♣ K J 9
  ♠ 9 7 3            N          ♠ J 10 8 5
  ♡ J 8 7 6 3               ♡ K 9 4
  ◇ 4 3         W       E     ◇ A 7
  ♣ A 8 4            S          ♣ 10 6 3 2
               ♠ A 2
               ♡ A 10 5
               ◇ K Q J 9 6
               ♣ Q 7 5
```

The play
South should play a low heart from dummy, ensuring two tricks
from the suit. South covers whatever card East plays and then
knocks out the ◇A. East will no doubt continue hearts (best),
but declarer makes: 4 diamonds, 2 hearts and 3 spades.

The principle
Avoid squandering your honour cards. In the above example it
would be fatal to contribute the ♡Q on the first trick (a play that
would be correct without the ten in the South hand) as this would
result in swift defeat. As long as you play low from dummy you
are assured of two tricks from the suit – regardless of the distribution. Contrast hand 5, where declarer did not have the ♡10, a
vital difference.

12. E-W game; dealer South.   Contract: 7S by South.

♠ 5 4 3
♡ 9 7 4 2
◇ K J 8 5
♣ K Q

♠ A K Q J 10 6
♡ A 5 3
◇ A Q
♣ A 6

The bidding

S	N
2♣	2 NT
3♠	3 NT
4 NT	5♣
5 NT	6♡
7♠	

West leads the knave of clubs. How should South plan the play?

12. E-W game; dealer South.   Contract: 7S by South.

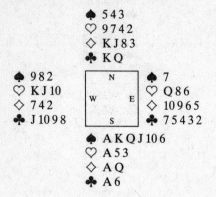

```
              ♠ 5 4 3
              ♡ 9 7 4 2
              ◇ K J 8 3
              ♣ K Q
   ♠ 9 8 2         N         ♠ 7
   ♡ K J 10                  ♡ Q 8 6
   ◇ 7 4 2    W       E      ◇ 10 9 6 5
   ♣ J 10 9 8      S         ♣ 7 5 4 3 2
              ♠ A K Q J 10 6
              ♡ A 5 3
              ◇ A Q
              ♣ A 6
```

The play
South should appreciate that he must overtake the ♣Q with the ace, since he needs a club entry in dummy to enjoy the diamonds. The play goes: ♣Q overtaken by ♣A, three rounds of trumps, followed by the ◇AQ. South now enters dummy with the ♣K and disposes of his two losing hearts on dummy's DKJ. Declarer makes: 6 spades, 4 diamonds, 2 clubs and 1 heart.

The principle
Before playing to the first trick be sure to make a *complete* plan. In this instance, if you fail to preserve your one and only entry to dummy you will be defeated.

13. Game all; dealer North.   Contract: 4H by South.

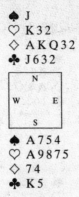

♠ J
♡ K 3 2
◇ A K Q 3 2
♣ J 6 3 2

♠ A 7 5 4
♡ A 9 8 7 5
◇ 7 4
♣ K 5

The bidding

S	W	N	E
—	—	1◇	Pass
1♡	1♠	2♡	Pass
4♡	Pass	Pass	Pass

West leads the king of spades. How should South plan the play?

13. Game all; dealer North.   Contract: 4H by South.

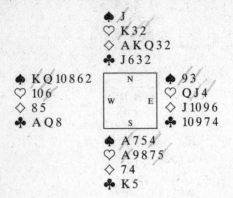

♠ J
♡ K 3 2
◇ A K Q 3 2
♣ J 6 3 2

♠ K Q 10 8 6 2
♡ 10 6
◇ 8 5
♣ A Q 8

♠ 9 3
♡ Q J 4
◇ J 10 9 6
♣ 10 9 7 4

♠ A 7 5 4
♡ A 9 8 7 5
◇ 7 4
♣ K 5

The play

South should win with the ♠A, cash the ♡AK and then play on diamonds, discarding a spade on the third top diamond. He ruffs a diamond, ruffs a spade and plays the thirteenth diamond, throwing his last spade. East can ruff this trick if he likes, but South makes: 4 hearts, 1 spade, 1 spade ruff and 4 diamonds (or 5 hearts and 3 diamonds).

The principle

It is often expedient to leave one master trump at large. This play preserves an extra trump for declarer, sometimes in both hands. It also affords him the 'tempo' – that is to say he keeps the lead. In the above case declarer would fail if he drew more than two rounds of trumps. Notice also the timing: declarer delays ruffing a spade in dummy until the ruff gives him access to dummy's established diamond.

14. Love all; dealer South.   Contract: 4H by South.

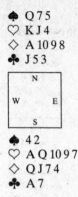

♠ Q 7 5
♡ K J 4
♦ A 10 9 8
♣ J 5 3

♠ 4 2
♡ A Q 10 9 7
♦ Q J 7 4
♣ A 7

The bidding

S	W	N	E
1♡	1♠	2♦	Pass
3♦	Pass	3♡	Pass
4♡	Pass	Pass	Pass

West leads the ace of spades, East following with the three. How should South plan the play?

Deception

14. Love all; dealer South.   Contract: 4H by South.

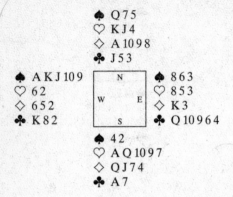

```
                    ♠ Q75
                    ♡ KJ4
                    ◇ A1098
                    ♣ J53
   ♠ AKJ109      N            ♠ 863
   ♡ 62                       ♡ 853
   ◇ 652      W       E       ◇ K3
   ♣ K82                      ♣ Q10964
                    S
                    ♠ 42
                    ♡ AQ1097
                    ◇ QJ74
                    ♣ A7
```

The play
Declarer should play the four of spades on the ace. This small deception may encourage West to continue the suit (playing his partner for ♠3 2) instead of finding the killing switch to a club. Declarer would then make: 5 hearts, 1 spade, 1 club and 3 diamonds.

The principle
When you want the opponents to continue their suit, follow the simple rule of starting an echo, just as you do in defence. If you want to discourage your opponents, play your lowest card. Obviously you'll give the show away if you stop and think and then play. However, the rule is so simple that, once you know it, it hardly needs any deliberation.

In the above hand, if West is persuaded to continue spades he will see on the next round that you have tricked him, but the club switch will now be too late. You will discard the ♣7 on the ♠Q, and your only losers will be the ♠AK and ◇K.

15. Game all; dealer South.   Contract: 6H by South.

♠ A 8 6 3
♡ K J 10 5
♢ A 8 6 5
♣ 3

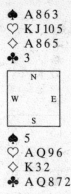

♠ 5
♡ A Q 9 6
♢ K 3 2
♣ A Q 8 7 2

The bidding

S	N
1♣	1♢
1♡	3♠*
4♣	4♢
6♡	

(*Agrees hearts and pin-points spade control)

West leads the king of spades. How should South plan the play?

15. Game all; dealer South.   Contract: 6H by South.

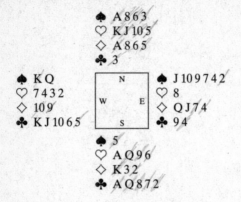

```
              ♠ A 8 6 3
              ♡ K J 10 5
              ◇ A 8 6 5
              ♣ 3
  ♠ K Q           N           ♠ J 10 9 7 4 2
  ♡ 7 4 3 2                   ♡ 8
  ◇ 10 9      W       E       ◇ Q J 7 4
  ♣ K J 10 6 5      S         ♣ 9 4
              ♠ 5
              ♡ A Q 9 6
              ◇ K 3 2
              ♣ A Q 8 7 2
```

The play
South sees that he was lucky to escape a trump lead, but he still has only four sure tricks outside hearts: ◇AK, ♠A, ♣A. He should, therefore, win the ♠A, cash the ◇AK and the ♣A, and ruff a club with the ♡5. He now ruffs a spade with the ♡6 and continues ruffing clubs and spades alternately. By this process he will make 8 trump tricks, 2 diamonds, 1 club and 1 spade.

The principle
Whenever there are shortages in both hands you should consider the possibility of a crossruff, which can produce a rich harvest of trump tricks. Where possible, cash your side winners before embarking on the crossruff. In the above hand, if declarer neglects to cash his diamond winners immediately the contract will fail, because West will be able to discard a diamond on the third round of spades; unable to draw trumps, South will later see one of his vital diamond winners ruffed.

16. Love all; dealer North.   Contract: 3 NT by South.

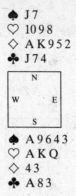

♠ J 7
♡ 10 9 8
♢ A K 9 5 2
♣ J 7 4

♠ A 9 6 4 3
♡ A K Q
♢ 4 3
♣ A 8 3

The bidding

N	S
Pass	1♠
2♢	2 NT
3 NT	

West leads the five of spades to dummy's knave and East's king. How should South plan the play?

Ducking to maintain contact

16. Love all; dealer North.   Contract: 3 NT by South.

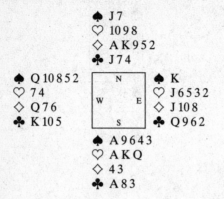

```
                ♠ J 7
                ♡ 10 9 8
                ◇ A K 9 5 2
                ♣ J 7 4
  ♠ Q 10 8 5 2      N        ♠ K
  ♡ 7 4                      ♡ J 6 5 3 2
  ◇ Q 7 6      W       E     ◇ J 10 8
  ♣ K 10 5          S        ♣ Q 9 6 2
                ♠ A 9 6 4 3
                ♡ A K Q
                ◇ 4 3
                ♣ A 8 3
```

The play

It is too great a risk to duck the spade, and perhaps get a club switch, so declarer takes the trick with the ♠A. With only seven tricks on top he needs two extra tricks from diamonds, and this requires the suit to break 3–3. However, if he now plays ◇AK and another, he will be unable to return to dummy to enjoy the other two (if they *are* winners). Therefore he starts by playing a low diamond from each hand. On regaining the lead, he plays a second diamond to dummy's ace, which enables him to collect nine tricks: 4 diamonds, 3 hearts, 1 spade and 1 club.

The principle

Sometimes you wish to enjoy a long suit but the entries are limited. When this is the case it is often possible to preserve the communications by ducking the first round. In the above example the 3–3 break in diamonds, although against the odds, represented declarer's only realistic chance.

17. Game all; dealer South.   Contract: 4H by South.

♠ 10 5 2
♡ J 8 6
◇ A K 10 9
♣ A 9 4

```
      N
  W       E
      S
```

♠ 4 3
♡ A K Q 5
◇ Q J 8 5
♣ K 5 3

The bidding

S	W	N	E
1♡	1♠	2◇	Pass
3◇	Pass	3♡	Pass
4♡	Pass	Pass	Pass

West leads the ace, king and queen of spades. How should South plan the play?

Refusing the ruff

17. Game all; dealer South.   Contract: 4H by South.

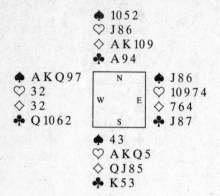

```
              ♠ 10 5 2
              ♡ J 8 6
              ◇ A K 10 9
              ♣ A 9 4
♠ A K Q 9 7        N        ♠ J 8 6
♡ 3 2                      ♡ 10 9 7 4
◇ 3 2         W       E     ◇ 7 6 4
♣ Q 10 6 2        S        ♣ J 8 7
              ♠ 4 3
              ♡ A K Q 5
              ◇ Q J 8 5
              ♣ K 5 3
```

The play

South should refuse to ruff the third round of spades; he should discard his inevitable club loser instead. South will win the next lead (if West continues spades, dummy ruffs low, and if East should overruff South takes the trick with a trump honour), draw trumps and cash his winners. He makes: 4 hearts, 4 diamonds and 2 clubs.

The principle

When you are given the opportunity to ruff something, consider the advantages of refusing the offer and discarding a loser instead. In the above hand, declarer has no parking place for his losing club so he might just as well dispose of it rather than weaken his trump holding. On this occasion it is the only way to make the contract. This is a frequent way out of trouble when you have a 4–3 trump suit.

18. Game all; dealer South.   Contract: 4H by South.

♠ 8 3
♡ K 9 5 3
♢ J 7 5
♣ A J 8 5

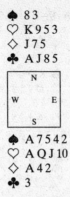

♠ A 7 5 4 2
♡ A Q J 10
♢ A 4 2
♣ 3

The bidding

S	N
1♠	1 NT
2♡	3♡
4♡	

West leads the king of clubs. How should South plan the play?

18. Game all; dealer South.   Contract: 4H by South.

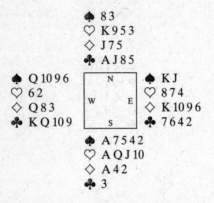

                ♠ 83
                ♡ K 9 5 3
                ◇ J 7 5
                ♣ A J 8 5

♠ Q 10 9 6   ♠ K J
♡ 6 2   ♡ 8 7 4
◇ Q 8 3   ◇ K 10 9 6
♣ K Q 10 9   ♣ 7 6 4 2

                ♠ A 7 5 4 2
                ♡ A Q J 10
                ◇ A 4 2
                ♣ 3

The play
South should take the first trick with dummy's ♣A and play the
ace and another spade. Suppose East switches to a diamond.
South wins, ruffs a spade high, re-enters his own hand with a
heart, and ruffs a second spade high. Dummy's last heart enables
South to get back to his own hand to draw the last trump and
cash his established spade winner. Declarer makes: 4 hearts, 2
spades, 2 spade ruffs and the two minor suit aces.

The principle
When you are short of tricks (in the above hand there are only
seven on top) and have a long side suit, consider setting it up by
ruffing the losing cards. Entries may present a problem, so plot
your course to and fro before you play to the first trick.

19. Game all; dealer North.   Contract: 3 NT by South.

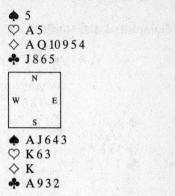

♠ 5
♡ A 5
♢ A Q 10 9 5 4
♣ J 8 6 5

♠ A J 6 4 3
♡ K 6 3
♢ K
♣ A 9 3 2

The bidding

N	S
1♢	1♠
2♢	3 NT

West leads the queen of hearts. How should South plan the play?

19. Game all; dealer North.   Contract: 3 NT by South.

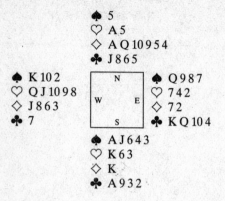

```
              ♠ 5
              ♡ A 5
              ◇ A Q 10 9 5 4
              ♣ J 8 6 5
  ♠ K 10 2          N          ♠ Q 9 8 7
  ♡ Q J 10 9 8             ♡ 7 4 2
  ◇ J 8 6 3      W     E      ◇ 7 2
  ♣ 7               S          ♣ K Q 10 4
              ♠ A J 6 4 3
              ♡ K 6 3
              ◇ K
              ♣ A 9 3 2
```

The play
South should win the heart lead in his own hand, play the ◇K
and overtake with the ◇A. He now plays the ◇Q followed by
the ◇10, forcing out the ◇J. South makes his contract with: 5
diamonds, 2 hearts, 1 spade and 1 club.

The principle
It is sometimes necessary to sacrifice high honour cards in order
to give oneself the best chance of establishing a long suit. In the
above hand the recommended line will succeed provided the
diamonds are no worse than J x x x in one hand. Should declarer
attempt to cash the ◇K separately, the contract will fail for lack
of entries. Obviously if you needed six diamond tricks to make
your contract you would have to hope that the suit divided, or
the knave fell in two rounds. This example illustrates how vital it
is to count your tricks.

20. Love all; dealer South.   Contract: 4H by South.

♠ 4 3 2
♡ A 6
♢ 8 7 3
♣ K Q J 10 8

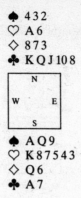

♠ A Q 9
♡ K 8 7 5 4 3
♢ Q 6
♣ A 7

The bidding

S	W	N	E
1♡	2♢	3♣	Pass
3♢	Pass	3♡	Pass
4♡	Pass	Pass	Pass

West leads the ace, king and knave of diamonds. How should South plan the play?

20. Love all; dealer South.   Contract: 4H by South.

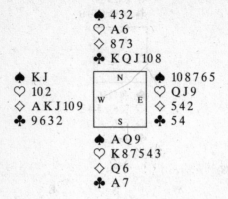

♠ 4 3 2
♡ A 6
♢ 8 7 3
♣ K Q J 10 8

♠ K J
♡ 10 2
♢ A K J 10 9
♣ 9 6 3 2

♠ 10 8 7 6 5
♡ Q J 9
♢ 5 4 2
♣ 5 4

♠ A Q 9
♡ K 8 7 5 4 3
♢ Q 6
♣ A 7

The play
South should ruff the third round of diamonds and play the ace, king and another heart, giving the opposition their trump trick at once. East wins and returns a spade, but declarer goes up with the ace, cashes the ♣A and continues clubs, discarding his two spade losers. He makes: 5 hearts, 1 spade and 4 clubs.

The principle
When you have a long, solid suit that you wish to cash but have no outside entries, you must remove the one sting that the opposition may have to hurt you – their trumps. In the above hand, if South neglects to give East his ♡Q, East will use it to trump the third round of clubs and the contract will fail. (However, see hand 13.)

21. E-W game; dealer South.   Contract: 4H by South.

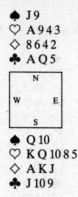

```
            ♠ J 9
            ♡ A 9 4 3
            ◇ 8 6 4 2
            ♣ A Q 5
```

```
            ♠ Q 10
            ♡ K Q 10 8 5
            ◇ A K J
            ♣ J 10 9
```

The bidding

S	N
1♡	3♡
4♡	

West leads the two of spades. East wins with the ace and returns the four to West's king. West switches to a club which is won by East's king. East now plays the three of diamonds. How should declarer plan the play?

Precaution play

21. E-W game; dealer South.   Contract: 4H by South.

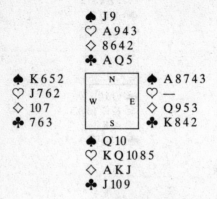

```
            ♠ J 9
            ♡ A 9 4 3
            ◇ 8 6 4 2
            ♣ A Q 5
♠ K 6 5 2                      ♠ A 8 7 4 3
♡ J 7 6 2      N               ♡ —
◇ 10 7      W     E            ◇ Q 9 5 3
♣ 7 6 3         S             ♣ K 8 4 2
            ♠ Q 10
            ♡ K Q 10 8 5
            ◇ A K J
            ♣ J 10 9
```

The play

The diamond finesses will presumably have to be taken eventually – but there is no need to risk it at this point. The ◇A wins
trick four, and it is now time to tackle the trumps, employing a
precaution play. South starts by playing the ♡K to cater for
either opponent's holding all the missing trumps. He continues
with the ♡Q and a heart to dummy's A9 to complete the task.
When the finesse of the knave of diamonds succeeds declarer is
home with: 5 hearts, 3 diamonds and 2 clubs.

The principle

When holding all the missing top cards down to the nine, except
the knave, and with the honours split, you should start by
playing a top honour from the hand containing two of the top
three honours. You will then be in a position to pick up J x x x in
either opponent's hand. (Compare with hand 46.)

22. Love all; dealer North.   Contract: 3 NT by South.

♠ 75
♡ A K 9 6 5
♢ A Q J 8
♣ 4 2

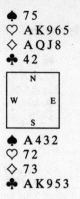

♠ A 4 3 2
♡ 7 2
♢ 7 3
♣ A K 9 5 3

The bidding

N	S
1♡	1♠
2♢	2 NT
3 NT	

West leads the queen of clubs, East following with the six. How should South plan the play?

Deception

22. Love all; dealer North.   Contract: 3 NT by South.

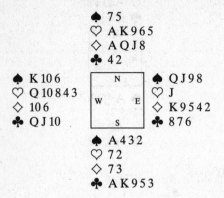

```
               ♠ 7 5
               ♡ A K 9 6 5
               ◇ A Q J 8
               ♣ 4 2
   ♠ K 10 6                   ♠ Q J 9 8
   ♡ Q 10 8 4 3      N        ♡ J
   ◇ 10 6        W       E    ◇ K 9 5 4 2
   ♣ Q J 10         S        ♣ 8 7 6
               ♠ A 4 3 2
               ♡ 7 2
               ◇ 7 3
               ♣ A K 9 5 3
```

The play

Having concealed his long suit in the bidding, South has been rewarded with a favourable lead, but he requires the technique to take advantage of this development. South should play the ♣5 on the ♣Q, concealing the ♣3, and hope that West supposes his partner has made an encouraging signal. If West continues clubs, South will be able to cash 4 of them. Although the diamond finesse loses, this suit will still provide 2 tricks; 2 more tricks from hearts and 1 from spades complete the required total of 9.

The principle

As in hand 14, South deceitfully starts an echo. In the above example, if South wins the first club and returns the suit, West will appreciate that he has not struck gold and may find the killing switch – a spade.

23. Game all; dealer South.   Contract: 3 NT by South.

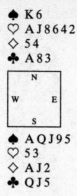

                    ♠ K 6
                    ♡ A J 8 6 4 2
                    ◇ 5 4
                    ♣ A 8 3

                    ♠ A Q J 9 5
                    ♡ 5 3
                    ◇ A J 2
                    ♣ Q J 5

The bidding

        S   N
        1♠   2♡
        2 NT   3 NT

West leads the king of diamonds. How should South plan the play?

The Bath Coup

23. Game all; dealer South.   Contract: 3 NT by South.

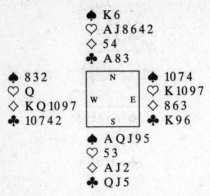

```
                ♠ K 6
                ♡ A J 8 6 4 2
                ◇ 5 4
                ♣ A 8 3
  ♠ 8 3 2          N          ♠ 10 7 4
  ♡ Q                         ♡ K 10 9 7
  ◇ K Q 10 9 7   W   E        ◇ 8 6 3
  ♣ 10 7 4 2        S         ♣ K 9 6
                ♠ A Q J 9 5
                ♡ 5 3
                ◇ A J 2
                ♣ Q J 5
```

The play
South should refuse the ◇K (Bath Coup), forcing West to switch
or needlessly sacrifice a trick. Let us say he switches to a club.
East takes his king and returns a diamond, but now South has
nine tricks. He makes: 5 spades, 1 heart, 1 diamond and 2 clubs.
If West continues diamonds at trick two, declarer will make an
overtrick.

The principle
The Bath Coup, which dates from the early days of whist,
consists of a simple hold-up play when you have the ace in
combination with the knave. It offers the defender the choice of
continuing, and conceding an extra trick, or temporarily aban-
doning the suit. The play is equally effective when the ace and
knave are split as in the following diagram:

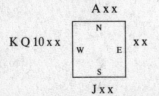

```
                A x x
                  N
  K Q 10 x x    W   E    x x
                  S
                J x x
```

The king is led, and declarer plays low from both hands.

24. Love all; dealer South.   Contract: 3 NT by South

♠ 754
♡ A K 10 6 3
♢ 976
♣ J 2

♠ A K J
♡ 74
♢ K J 3
♣ A K 10 9 8

The bidding

S	N
1♣	1♡
3 NT	

West leads the four of diamonds to East's queen. How should South plan the play?

24. Love all; dealer South.   Contract: 3 NT by South.

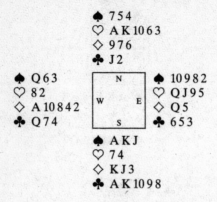

```
                    ♠ 7 5 4
                    ♡ A K 10 6 3
                    ◇ 9 7 6
                    ♣ J 2
    ♠ Q 6 3                         ♠ 10 9 8 2
    ♡ 8 2          N                ♡ Q J 9 5
    ◇ A 10 8 4 2  W   E             ◇ Q 5
    ♣ Q 7 4          S              ♣ 6 5 3
                    ♠ A K J
                    ♡ 7 4
                    ◇ K J 3
                    ♣ A K 10 9 8
```

The play
South should win the first trick with the ◇K, enter dummy with
the ♡A and play the ♣J. West can win this trick, but as the ◇J
is protected while West is on lead, declarer is safe. Declarer
makes at least nine tricks with 4 clubs, 1 diamond, 2 hearts and 2
spades.

The principle
When a vital decision has to be made in one suit the correct play
is often dictated by the distribution of another. In the above
hand the declarer must develop the club suit, which means
finessing through East. Therefore, if he wins the ◇K, the ◇J
will be protected should West win with the ♣Q.

25. Love all; dealer South.   Contract: 4H by South.

♠ 10 9
♡ 9 6 2
♢ A 8 6 4 2
♣ A K 9

♠ A 8
♡ A K Q J 4
♢ 7 5 3
♣ 5 3 2

The bidding

S	N
1♡	2♢
2♡	3♡
4♡	

West leads the queen of clubs. How should South plan the play? (As it happens 3 NT is laydown. Nevertheless you are saddled with the task of making 4H – with 'A hundred honours, partner'.)

The double duck

25. Love all; dealer South.   Contract: 4H by South.

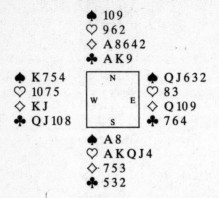

```
              ♠ 10 9
              ♡ 9 6 2
              ◇ A 8 6 4 2
              ♣ A K 9
  ♠ K 7 5 4          ♠ Q J 6 3 2
  ♡ 10 7 5      N    ♡ 8 3
  ◇ K J     W     E  ◇ Q 10 9
  ♣ Q J 10 8     S   ♣ 7 6 4
              ♠ A 8
              ♡ A K Q J 4
              ◇ 7 5 3
              ♣ 5 3 2
```

The play

With nine tricks on top (four losers) declarer needs to establish one extra trick for his contract, and it can only come from diamonds. He should win the club lead, draw trumps and play a low diamond from each hand. The defence will no doubt knock out the other top club, but declarer is still a move ahead and plays a second low diamond from each hand. The defence can cash their club winner, but as the diamond suit is now established declarer can dispose of his losing spade. Declarer makes: 5 hearts, 2 clubs, 2 diamonds and 1 spade.

The principle

Establishing a long suit is a common method of providing extra winners. When entries are short consider ducking one, or even two, early rounds in order to maintain communication.

26. Love all; dealer South.   Contract: 5C by South.

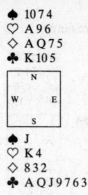

♠ 1074
♡ A96
♢ A Q 7 5
♣ K 10 5

♠ J
♡ K 4
♢ 8 3 2
♣ A Q J 9 7 6 3

The bidding

S	W	N	E
1♣	1♠	2♢	2♠
3♣	Pass	5♣	Pass
Pass	Pass		

West leads the ace of spades followed by the king of spades. South ruffs and tests the trumps, finding that East has all three. How should he plan the play?

26. Love all; dealer South.   Contract: 5C by South.

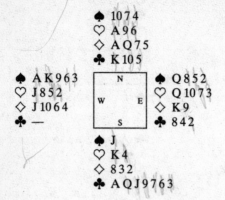

```
              ♠ 10 7 4
              ♡ A 9 6
              ◇ A Q 7 5
              ♣ K 10 5
 ♠ A K 9 6 3        N        ♠ Q 8 5 2
 ♡ J 8 5 2                   ♡ Q 10 7 3
 ◇ J 10 6 4    W       E     ◇ K 9
 ♣ —                S        ♣ 8 4 2
              ♠ J
              ♡ K 4
              ◇ 8 3 2
              ♣ A Q J 9 7 6 3
```

The play

Declarer has ten tricks on top. He needs one more for his contract, which presumably must come from diamonds. He should draw trumps, finishing in dummy, and play the ◇5. Yes, away from the AQ. As declarer is leading up to the closed hand, East may be anxious about his ◇K and play it at once. If that happens South's problems are over. He can spread his cards and claim the remainder of the tricks.

The principle

When you hold three small cards opposite AQxx in dummy, unless there are other considerations, it costs nothing to play low from the table. This play puts the defender on your right under pressure, and he may well make a mistake (sometimes declarer has the guarded knave and, for various reasons, decides to make this play). If the finesse is right, it can still be taken on the next round.

27. N-S game; dealer North.   Contract: 6S by South.

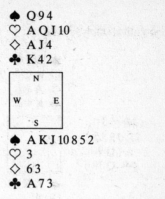

♠ Q 9 4
♡ A Q J 10
◇ A J 4
♣ K 4 2

♠ A K J 10 8 5 2
♡ 3
◇ 6 3
♣ A 7 3

The bidding

N	S
1♡	1♠ (SPADE)
2 NT	3♣ (CLUBS)
3♠	4 NT
5♡	5 NT
6◇	6♠

West leads the two of diamonds. How should South plan the play?

27. N-S game; dealer North.   Contract: 6S by South.

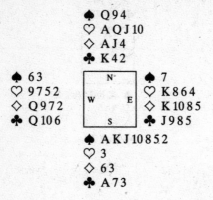

♠ Q 9 4
♡ A Q J 10
◇ A J 4
♣ K 4 2

♠ 6 3
♡ 9 7 5 2
◇ Q 9 7 2
♣ Q 10 6

♠ 7
♡ K 8 6 4
◇ K 10 8 5
♣ J 9 8 5

♠ A K J 10 8 5 2
♡ 3
◇ 6 3
♣ A 7 3

The play

South should win the opening lead with the ◇A, draw trumps and play a heart to the ace. He continues with the ♡Q, and now it does not matter who has the ♡K. If East plays low, South discards his last diamond. If West wins this trick, the losing club can be discarded on the ♡J. If East has the ♡K, as in the above diagram, the declarer will be able to take all thirteen tricks. He makes: 7 spades, 3 hearts, 1 diamond and 2 clubs.

The principle

If declarer can afford to lose to a missing honour, a ruffing finesse is often a safer play than a straightforward finesse because he can discard a loser when the honour card is not covered. In the above hand, if South takes the normal finesse, playing West for the ♡K, he will lose two tricks – a heart and a diamond. The ruffing finesse makes the contract a certainty.

28. Love all; dealer North.   Contract: 4S by South.

♠ J96
♡ A K 94
♢ A 10 6
♣ 10 4 2

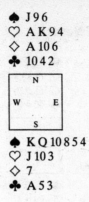

♠ K Q 10 8 5 4
♡ J 10 3
♢ 7
♣ A 5 3

The bidding

S	W	N	E
—	—	1 NT	2◇
4♠	Pass	Pass	Pass

West leads the king of clubs. How should South plan the play?

Hold up in a suit contract

28. Love all; dealer North.   Contract: 4S by South.

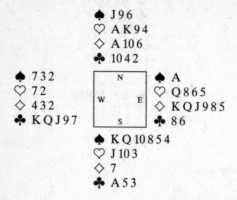

```
              ♠ J 9 6
              ♡ A K 9 4
              ♢ A 10 6
              ♣ 10 4 2
♠ 7 3 2          N          ♠ A
♡ 7 2                       ♡ Q 8 6 5
♢ 4 3 2      W     E        ♢ K Q J 9 8 5
♣ K Q J 9 7      S          ♣ 8 6
              ♠ K Q 10 8 5 4
              ♡ J 10 3
              ♢ 7
              ♣ A 5 3
```

The play

South should refuse the first club, win the continuation and knock out the ♠A. He wins the diamond switch in dummy and draws the last two trumps, ending in his hand. Next, he leads the ♡J, running it when West plays low. East wins this trick, but dummy's fourth heart provides a parking-place for South's losing club. Declarer makes: 5 spades, 3 hearts and the 2 minor-suit aces.

The principle

The hold-up in a suit contract is a valuable weapon. Frequently declarer will employ the hold-up to cut the enemy communications. On the above hand, if South wins the first club the defence will be able to cash 1 spade, 2 clubs and 1 heart (there is a small risk that West might hold six clubs, in which case the recommended line will fail unless the heart finesse is right or – as in the actual case – East has the singleton ♠A).

29. Love all; dealer North.   Contract: 6S by South.

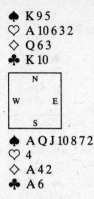

♠ K 9 5
♡ A 10 6 3 2
♢ Q 6 3
♣ K 10

♠ A Q J 10 8 7 2
♡ 4
♢ A 4 2
♣ A 6

The bidding

N	S
1 NT	3♠
4♠	4 NT
5♢	6♠

West leads the ten of diamonds. South tries the queen from dummy, but East plays the king. How should South plan the play?

Developing a suit by ruffing

29. Love all; dealer North. Contract: 6S by South.

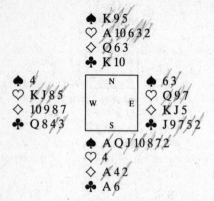

```
            ♠ K 9 5
            ♡ A 10 6 3 2
            ◇ Q 6 3
            ♣ K 10
♠ 4                          ♠ 6 3
♡ K J 8 5      N             ♡ Q 9 7
◇ 10 9 8 7   W   E           ◇ K J 5
♣ Q 8 4 3      S             ♣ J 9 7 5 2
            ♠ A Q J 10 8 7 2
            ♡ 4
            ◇ A 4 2
            ♣ A 6
```

The play

South should win the first trick with the ◇A and play a top spade from his hand. The ♡A and a heart ruff are followed by a spade to dummy's nine and a second heart ruff. Now a spade to dummy's king and a third heart ruff establishes the ten of hearts. The ♣K is the final entry to dummy to cash the ♡10 and discard a losing diamond. Declarer concedes one diamond trick at the end – the only loser.

The principle

When forming your plan, always remember that a long suit is invariably a potential source of extra tricks. In the above hand declarer has to be careful with entries. For example, he cannot draw two rounds of trumps before starting on the hearts. If he does he will find that he has established the extra heart winner – but lacks an entry to enjoy it.

30. Love all; dealer South.   Contract: 3 NT by South.

♠ A K 10 8 5
♡ 7 5 2
♢ 9 3
♣ A 8 4

♠ 7 4
♡ A K 3
♢ Q J 10 8 7
♣ K Q 10

The bidding

S	N
1♢	1♠
1 NT	3 NT

West leads the six of hearts to East's knave. How should South plan the play?

Hold up with double stopper

30. Love all; dealer South.   Contract: 3 NT by South.

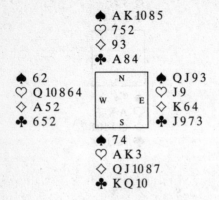

```
            ♠ A K 10 8 5
            ♡ 7 5 2
            ◇ 9 3
            ♣ A 8 4
♠ 6 2                          ♠ Q J 9 3
♡ Q 10 8 6 4      N            ♡ J 9
◇ A 5 2        W     E         ◇ K 6 4
♣ 6 5 2           S           ♣ J 9 7 3
            ♠ 7 4
            ♡ A K 3
            ◇ Q J 10 8 7
            ♣ K Q 10
```

The play
South should hold up his honours, allowing East to win the first
trick. South wins the heart continuation and plays a diamond. It
does not matter which defender wins this trick, as declarer can
win the next, knock out the second top diamond and claim ten
tricks. Note the difference if declarer makes the mistake of
winning the first heart; East wins trick two with the ◇K and
plays a second heart, permitting the defence to clear the suit.
West pounces on the next diamond and cashes his heart winners
– and that adds up to five tricks: 3 hearts and 2 diamonds.

The principle
Although two stoppers in the suit which the opponents have led
looks a substantial guard, one should consider the advantages of
holding up. Providing there is not a greater weakness elsewhere,
the hold-up is often the right play. This is especially true where
declarer has to dislodge two defensive tricks in *his* long suit.

31. Game all; dealer South.   Contract: 3 NT by South.

♠ Q9754
♡ J6
♢ J93
♣ K104

```
        N
   W         E
        S
```

♠ J32
♡ A103
♢ AQ104
♣ AQ9

The bidding

S	N
1♢	1♠
2 NT	3 NT

West leads the four of hearts to East's queen and South's ace. How should declarer continue, and in particular how should he play the diamonds?

Repeating the finesse

31. Game all; dealer South.   Contract: 3 NT by South.

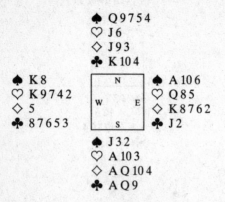

```
                        ♠ Q 9 7 5 4
                        ♡ J 6
                        ◇ J 9 3
                        ♣ K 10 4
        ♠ K 8                              ♠ A 10 6
        ♡ K 9 7 4 2          N            ♡ Q 8 5
        ◇ 5            W         E         ◇ K 8 7 6 2
        ♣ 8 7 6 5 3          S            ♣ J 2
                        ♠ J 3 2
                        ♡ A 10 3
                        ◇ A Q 10 4
                        ♣ A Q 9
```

The play
The first point to note is that declarer refrained from playing the
♡J at trick one. That would have been a silly thing to do because
as long as he played low he was certain to make *two* tricks in the
suit. (See hand 11 for a similar case.) The next point of technique
concerns the diamond finesse. Declarer enters dummy with the
♣K, but since there are no more sure entries to the North hand,
it is essential to start by playing the ◇9 rather than the knave.
Now it is possible to pick up four tricks in the suit. In his hand
with the ◇Q at trick five, declarer needs to establish one more
trick for his contract, so he plays a low heart to the knave. Thus
he makes: 4 diamonds, 3 clubs and 2 hearts.

The principle
When you need to repeat a finesse, be careful to play the
intermediate and honour cards in the right order. In the above
hand it is essential to play the ◇9 first, then the ◇J and finally
the ◇3.

32. Game all; dealer South.   Contract: 3 NT by South.

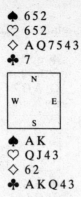

♠ 6 5 2
♥ 6 5 2
♦ A Q 7 5 4 3
♣ 7

♠ A K
♥ Q J 4 3
♦ 6 2
♣ A K Q 4 3

The bidding

S	N
1♣	1♦
2♥	3♦
3 NT	

West leads the four of spades. How should South plan the play?

32. Game all; dealer South. Contract: 3 NT by South.

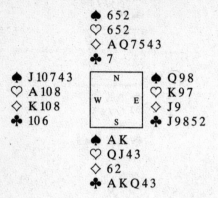

♠ 652
♡ 652
◇ A Q 7 5 4 3
♣ 7

♠ J 10 7 4 3
♡ A 10 8
◇ K 10 8
♣ 10 6

♠ Q 9 8
♡ K 9 7
◇ J 9
♣ J 9 8 5 2

♠ A K
♡ Q J 4 3
◇ 6 2
♣ A K Q 4 3

The play
South should play a diamond at trick two and duck it in dummy. On regaining the lead he plays his last diamond and takes the finesse. When the queen holds, and East follows, the rest is plain sailing. Declarer makes: 5 diamonds, 2 spades and 3 clubs.

The principle
When you wish to enjoy a long suit (usually in dummy) but entries are limited, consider ducking the first round completely, even if there is a finesse to be taken in the suit. On the above hand South will be defeated if he takes an immediate diamond finesse: although the finesse is successful, the run of the suit is impeded by West's third diamond.

33. Game all; dealer South.   Contract: 3 NT by South.

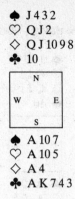

♠ J 4 3 2
♡ Q J 2
♢ Q J 10 9 8
♣ 10

♠ A 10 7
♡ A 10 5
♢ A 4
♣ A K 7 4 3

The bidding

S	N
1♣	1♢
3 NT	

West leads the four of hearts. How should South plan the play?

33. Game all; dealer South.   Contract: 3 NT by South.

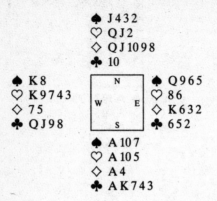

♠ J 4 3 2
♡ Q J 2
◇ Q J 10 9 8
♣ 10

♠ K 8
♡ K 9 7 4 3
◇ 7 5
♣ Q J 9 8

♠ Q 9 6 5
♡ 8 6
◇ K 6 3 2
♣ 6 5 2

♠ A 10 7
♡ A 10 5
◇ A 4
♣ A K 7 4 3

The play
Declarer should contribute a low heart from dummy and –
whatever East plays – win in his own hand with the *ace*. The ace
and another diamond dislodges East's king (if not, declarer
continues the suit until the king wins). If East switches to a
spade, declarer ducks; if East switches to a club, declarer wins
and plays a heart. Eventually he must gain access to the dummy
via the ♡QJ, which will enable him to cash the remainder of his
diamonds. He makes: 1 spade, 2 hearts, 4 diamonds and 2 clubs.

The principle
Pause before playing to the first trick to ensure that your plan
is watertight. In this case the accent is on entries, or the lack
of them. You desperately need one in dummy to enjoy your
diamonds, which is why you must play a low heart from dummy
at trick one and win in your own hand with the ace.

34. Game all; dealer South.   Contract: 4S by South.

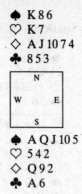

♠ K 8 6
♡ K 7
♢ A J 10 7 4
♣ 8 5 3

♠ A Q J 10 5
♡ 5 4 2
♢ Q 9 2
♣ A 6

The bidding

S	N
1♠	2♢
2♠	3♠
4♠	

West leads the four of clubs to East's king. How should South plan the play?

Protecting the weak holding

34. Game all; dealer South.   Contract: 4S by South.

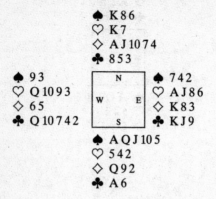

```
                    ♠ K 8 6
                    ♡ K 7
                    ◇ A J 10 7 4
                    ♣ 8 5 3
    ♠ 9 3              N           ♠ 7 4 2
    ♡ Q 10 9 3                     ♡ A J 8 6
    ◇ 6 5         W       E        ◇ K 8 3
    ♣ Q 10 7 4 2      S            ♣ K J 9
                    ♠ A Q J 10 5
                    ♡ 5 4 2
                    ◇ Q 9 2
                    ♣ A 6
```

The play
South should allow East's ♣K to win the first trick. As long as West cannot regain the lead the ♡K is protected and the diamond finesse can be taken in safety. South wins the club continuation, draws trumps and takes the diamond finesse; although this loses, declarer makes: 5 spades, 4 diamonds and 1 club.

The principle
One of the uses of the hold-up play is to protect a fragile holding by ensuring that only the non-dangerous hand is on lead. On the hand in the diagram, should South win the first club trick, the defence could take 1 club, 1 diamond and 2 hearts.

35. Game all; dealer South.   Contract: 6C by South.

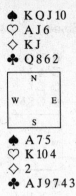

♠ K Q J 10
♡ A J 6
♢ K J
♣ Q 8 6 2

♠ A 7 5
♡ K 10 4
♢ 2
♣ A J 9 7 4 3

The bidding

S	N
1♣	2♠
3♣	4♣
4♠	4 NT
5♡	6♣

West leads the ten of diamonds to dummy's knave and East's queen. East continues with the ace of diamonds. How should South plan the play?

Finessing with the right card

35. Game all; dealer South.   Contract: 6C by South.

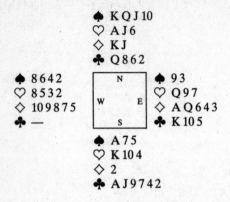

```
             ♠ K Q J 10
             ♡ A J 6
             ◇ K J
             ♣ Q 8 6 2
♠ 8 6 4 2        N        ♠ 9 3
♡ 8 5 3 2                 ♡ Q 9 7
◇ 10 9 8 7 5   W   E      ◇ A Q 6 4 3
♣ —              S        ♣ K 10 5
             ♠ A 7 5
             ♡ K 10 4
             ◇ 2
             ♣ A J 9 7 4 2
```

The play
Declarer should ruff the diamond return, enter dummy with the
♡A and play the ♣Q, running it if East does not cover. If East
plays the ♣K on the queen, the ♣10 can be picked up by a
second simple finesse. Of course, declarer intends to finesse in
trumps, in deference to the odds, but by playing the queen he
can restrict his losses to none when East holds K10x – something
he could not do if he played a low club to the knave.

The principle
When finessing it is often important to consider *which* card to
play first. With ten cards between the combined hands, missing
K10x, it is correct to play the queen first (or the knave first if the
holding is Jxxx opposite AQ9xxx), since this play cannot cost.
Even when the K10x are all on the wrong side, the play of the
queen gives nothing away – the defence will still make precisely
one trick. But the advantage is apparent when the cards are
distributed as in the hand above.

36. Game all; dealer South.   Contract: 4H by South.

♠ A K 10 8 6
♡ 4
♢ K 9 7
♣ 9 7 5 4

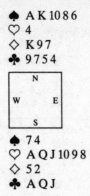

♠ 7 4
♡ A Q J 10 9 8
♢ 5 2
♣ A Q J

The bidding

S	N
1♡	1♠
3♡	3 NT
4♡	

West leads the queen of diamonds, dummy's king losing to
East's ace. South ruffs the third round of diamonds and enters
dummy with a spade. How should he continue?

36. Game all; dealer South.   Contract: 4H by South.

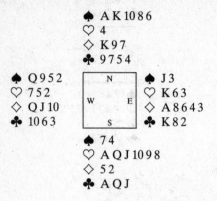

```
              ♠ A K 10 8 6
              ♡ 4
              ◇ K 9 7
              ♣ 9 7 5 4
  ♠ Q 9 5 2      N       ♠ J 3
  ♡ 7 5 2                ♡ K 6 3
  ◇ Q J 10   W     E     ◇ A 8 6 4 3
  ♣ 10 6 3      S        ♣ K 8 2
              ♠ 7 4
              ♡ A Q J 10 9 8
              ◇ 5 2
              ♣ A Q J
```

The play

Declarer should take the club finesse at trick five, and when the
knave holds he should play the ♡AQ. He ruffs the diamond
continuation, draws trumps and enters dummy with the ♠K to
finesse clubs once more. He makes: 5 hearts, 2 spades and 3
clubs.

Why should declarer reject the trump finesse in favour of the
club finesse? The point is that even if the trump finesse is
'successful' South will only be able to avoid a trump loser in the
unlikely case of the king's being doubleton. If the club finesse is
right, however, the suit can be picked up without loss.

The principle

When limited entries enforce a choice of finesse, be sure to select
the finesse that offers the greater chance of profit. In the above
hand, if you take the club finesse all you are asking is for the king
to be with East. If you take the heart finesse you are asking for
the king to be with East *and* for it to fall on the second round.

37. Game all; dealer North.   Contract: 3 NT by South.

♠ A K Q
♡ 6 5
◇ A K Q 7 4
♣ A Q 6

♠ 7 5 3 2
♡ A 8
◇ 5 2
♣ 8 5 4 3 2

The bidding

N	S
2♣	2◇
3◇	3 NT

West leads the four of hearts to East's king. How should South plan the play?

37. Game all; dealer North.   Contract: 3 NT by South.

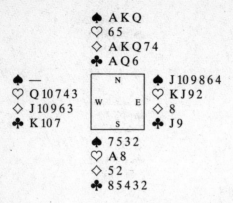

```
              ♠ A K Q
              ♡ 6 5
              ◇ A K Q 7 4
              ♣ A Q 6
 ♠ —                        ♠ J 10 9 8 6 4
 ♡ Q 10 7 4 3               ♡ K J 9 2
 ◇ J 10 9 6 3              ◇ 8
 ♣ K 10 7                   ♣ J 9
              ♠ 7 5 3 2
              ♡ A 8
              ◇ 5 2
              ♣ 8 5 4 3 2
```

The play
Declarer should take the second heart and play a small club towards dummy, contributing the queen when West plays low. When the club finesse wins, declarer cashes his tricks: 3 spades, 2 clubs, 3 diamonds and 1 heart.

The principle
As we shall see later, with a choice between playing for a suit to divide 3–3 and taking a simple finesse, it is often possible to try both. Here, however, South has a simple choice: should he finesse the ♣Q now or never? In such cases, you should always take the finesse (assuming there is no opposition bidding to influence your calculations). The reason is mathematical. The finesse is a 50 per cent chance whereas six outstanding cards will be divided 3–3 approximately 36 per cent of the time. Without getting involved in a mass of figures, a simple rule of thumb is this:

> With an even number of cards against you – expect the suit to break unevenly.

> With an odd number of cards against you – the suit is likely to divide favourably.

38. Love all; dealer South.   Contract: 4S by South.

♠ Q 4
♡ J 4
♦ A Q J 8 4
♣ Q J 10 9

♠ K 8 7 5 3 2
♡ 7 5
♦ K 6
♣ A K 4

The bidding

S	N
1♠	2♦
2♠	3♣
3♦	3♠
4♠	

West cashes the king and queen of hearts and switches to the eight of clubs. How should South plan the play?

Play up to the honours

38. Love all; dealer South.   Contract: 4S by South.

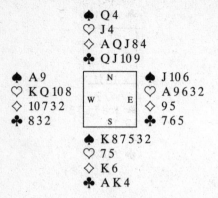

```
              ♠ Q 4
              ♡ J 4
              ◇ A Q J 8 4
              ♣ Q J 10 9
    ♠ A 9          N          ♠ J 10 6
    ♡ K Q 10 8            ♡ A 9 6 3 2
    ◇ 10 7 3 2  W    E     ◇ 9 5
    ♣ 8 3 2          S     ♣ 7 6 5
              ♠ K 8 7 5 3 2
              ♡ 7 5
              ◇ K 6
              ♣ A K 4
```

The play

Declarer should overtake the ♣9 with the ace and play a low spade towards dummy. West ducks (best), and the queen wins. Declarer returns the ♠4 towards the closed hand and plays low (this is known as the 'obligatory finesse' or the 'coup en blanc'). Once East has not taken the ♠A at trick four, declarer knows that West has that card, and the only hope is that he will now be forced to play it. When this is the case, declarer can then win any continuation and draw the outstanding trump. Declarer loses only 2 hearts and 1 spade.

The principle

Do not sacrifice honour cards unnecessarily. Play up to them rather than leading them. In the above example, if you were to make the mistake of leading either the king or queen of spades first, the contract would fail: West would play his ace, and East would later win a second trick in the suit. If West had held three spades the contract would have been doomed, no matter how you played the trump suit, but you must know how to take advantage of a favourable distribution.

39. E-W game; dealer South.   Contract: 4S by South.

♠ 9 6 4 2
♡ 9 7 4 3
♢ A 9 4
♣ K 6

♠ A Q 7 5 3
♡ Q 6
♢ K Q 2
♣ A Q 4

The bidding

S	N
1♠	2♠
4♠	

West leads the ace, king and eight of hearts to East's knave.
How should South plan the play?

39. E-W game; dealer South.   Contract: 4S by South.

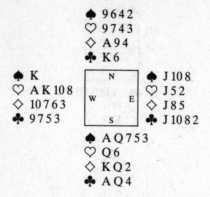

```
              ♠ 9 6 4 2
              ♡ 9 7 4 3
              ◇ A 9 4
              ♣ K 6
♠ K                        ♠ J 10 8
♡ A K 10 8                 ♡ J 5 2
◇ 10 7 6 3                 ◇ J 8 5
♣ 9 7 5 3                  ♣ J 10 8 2
              ♠ A Q 7 5 3
              ♡ Q 6
              ◇ K Q 2
              ♣ A Q 4
```

The play

Declarer should ruff the third heart and cash the ♠A. When the king falls he loses just one more trick to the ♠J. He makes: 4 spades, 3 diamonds and 3 clubs. Had the ♠K not fallen on the first round, declarer would have entered dummy with a minor suit winner and played a spade towards the closed hand, covering whatever card East played.

The principle

Playing the ace first from AQxxx opposite xxxx is a routine safety play to give yourself the maximum chance of restricting your losers in the suit to *one*. On this deal, declarer can afford to lose one trump, but not two. By playing the ace first he guards against West holding the bare king. Had declarer needed all five spade tricks, then he would have entered dummy and played towards the AQ, finessing the queen, his only chance now being a 2–2 split with the king on-side.

40. Love all; dealer South.   Contract: 4S by South.

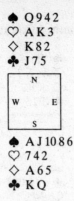

♠ Q 9 4 2
♡ A K 3
◇ K 8 2
♣ J 7 5

♠ A J 10 8 6
♡ 7 4 2
◇ A 6 5
♣ K Q

The bidding

S	W	N	E
1♠	2♡	4♠	Pass
Pass	Pass		

West leads the knave of hearts to dummy's ace and East's queen. How should South plan the play?

When not to finesse

40. Love all; dealer South.   Contract: 4S by South.

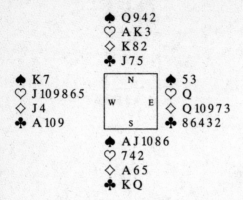

                    ♠ Q 9 4 2
                    ♡ A K 3
                    ◇ K 8 2
                    ♣ J 7 5
    ♠ K 7   ♠ 5 3
    ♡ J 10 9 8 6 5   ♡ Q
    ◇ J 4   ◇ Q 10 9 7 3
    ♣ A 10 9   ♣ 8 6 4 3 2
                    ♠ A J 10 8 6
                    ♡ 7 4 2
                    ◇ A 6 5
                    ♣ K Q

The play

With only three apparent losers (1 heart, 1 club and 1 spade, the losing diamond going on dummy's third club) declarer can afford to reject the spade finesse. This play avoids the danger of losing to West's ♠K and then suffering a heart ruff (East's ♡Q must surely be a singleton) to go one down. Nevertheless, at trick two declarer should play the ♠Q to tempt East to cover should he have the king. When East follows with the three, declarer plays the ace and another. He makes: 4 spades, 2 hearts, 2 diamonds and 2 clubs.

The principle

It will often be correct to take a finesse in order to gain an extra trick. However, it is most unwise to do so if an unsuccessful finesse courts the danger of a ruff which will then defeat the contract.

41. Game all; dealer South.   Contract: 4S by South.

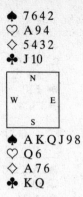

```
              ♠ 7 6 4 2
              ♡ A 9 4
              ◇ 5 4 3 2
              ♣ J 10
```

```
              ♠ A K Q J 9 8
              ♡ Q 6
              ◇ A 7 6
              ♣ K Q
```

The bidding

S	N
2♣	2 NT
3 NT	4♠

West leads the knave of hearts which is allowed to run to East's king. How should South plan the play?

41. Game all; dealer South.   Contract: 4S by South.

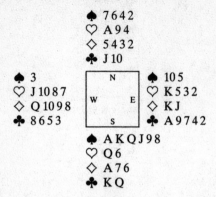

```
                    ♠ 7642
                    ♡ A94
                    ♢ 5432
                    ♣ J 10
      ♠ 3              N            ♠ 105
      ♡ J 1087                      ♡ K 532
      ♢ Q 1098      W     E        ♢ K J
      ♣ 8653                        ♣ A 9742
                        S
                    ♠ AKQJ98
                    ♡ Q6
                    ♢ A76
                    ♣ KQ
```

The play

Declarer must be careful to unblock the ♡Q on the king. He badly needs to discard a losing diamond (otherwise he will have to concede 1 heart, 1 club and 2 diamonds), but has only one entry to dummy. On regaining the lead, declarer draws trumps and then plays the ♡6, finessing dummy's nine. When the ♡9 holds, declarer cashes the ♡A and sheds a small diamond, claiming ten tricks. He makes: 6 spades, 2 hearts, 1 club and 1 diamond.

The principle

By throwing one high honour card on another, you can sometimes create an entry via a finesse. The advantage of this play is that it enables you to enjoy your full quota of winners in the suit led, while at the same time preserving the number of entries to the opposite hand. In this case West is likely to have the ♡10 in view of his lead. Once the KQJ have fallen together, the A9 afford both a finessing position and an entry to dummy which enable declarer to enjoy his two tricks in the suit. Of course, had there been one high spade in the dummy, even the ten, this unblocking play would not have been necessary.

42. Game all; dealer South.   Contract: 3 NT by South.

♠ A 5
♡ 10 5 3
♢ Q J 7 5
♣ A K 6 2

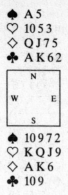

♠ 10 9 7 2
♡ K Q J 9
♢ A K 6
♣ 10 9

The bidding

S	N
1 NT	3 NT

West leads the six of spades. How should South plan the play?

42. Game all; dealer South.   Contract: 3 NT by South.

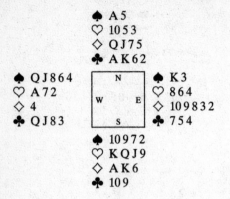

♠ A 5
♥ 10 5 3
♦ Q J 7 5
♣ A K 6 2

♠ Q J 8 6 4
♥ A 7 2
♦ 4
♣ Q J 8 3

♠ K 3
♥ 8 6 4
♦ 10 9 8 3 2
♣ 7 5 4

♠ 10 9 7 2
♥ K Q J 9
♦ A K 6
♣ 10 9

The play

Declarer should go in with dummy's ♠A in an endeavour to block the suit (West won't have underled *three* top honours – the KQJ). Declarer now knocks out the ♥A and thereafter must make: 3 hearts, 4 diamonds, 1 spade and 2 clubs. Note that East may unblock the ♠K on the ace, but the only difference is that South's spades are promoted to a second stop. If South plays a low spade from dummy at trick one the contract will fail, as the defence will make 4 spades and the ♥A.

The principle

Just as it is right to unblock your own suits to permit a free run, so it is correct to try and block the opponents'. In the above deal, if the spades are 4–3 it does not matter how declarer plays the suit, but if they are 5–2 it is highly probable that the doubleton includes an honour.

43. Love all; dealer South.   Contract: 4H by South.

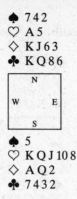

                    ♠ 742
                    ♡ A 5
                    ◇ K J 6 3
                    ♣ K Q 8 6

                    ♠ 5
                    ♡ K Q J 10 8
                    ◇ A Q 2
                    ♣ 7 4 3 2

The bidding

S	W	N	E
1♡	1♠	2◇	Pass
2♡	Pass	4♡	Pass
Pass	Pass		

West leads the ace and king of spades. How should South plan the play?

43. Love all; dealer South.   Contract: 4H by South.

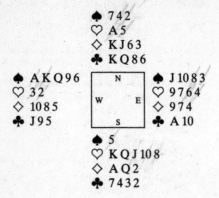

♠ 7 4 2
♥ A 5
♦ K J 6 3
♣ K Q 8 6

♠ A K Q 9 6
♥ 3 2
♦ 10 8 5
♣ J 9 5

♠ J 10 8 3
♥ 9 7 6 4
♦ 9 7 4
♣ A 10

♠ 5
♥ K Q J 10 8
♦ A Q 2
♣ 7 4 3 2

The play
Declarer should ruff the second spade, but defer drawing trumps. Failure to do this will leave him a trick short should the trumps divide 4–2. The correct play at trick three is a club to the king. Suppose East wins and plays another spade. This time South must refuse to ruff, discarding a club instead. Now whatever East plays declarer will win (a spade can be ruffed in dummy), draw trumps and claim ten tricks: 5 hearts, 4 diamonds and 1 club.

The principle
When the defence attempts to 'force' you to shorten your trumps – it may pay to refuse the ruff until dummy can accept it. Equally, you may have to postpone drawing trumps until you have set up a winner, or winners, in a side suit. In the meantime dummy's trumps prevent you from losing trump control. These two principles are clearly illustrated in the above hand.

44. Love all; dealer South.   Contract: 3 NT by South.

♠ K 9 6 4
♡ 7 4 3
♦ 9
♣ A Q 10 8 6

♠ A 8 3
♡ K J 6
♦ A K Q 5
♣ J 9 5

The bidding

S	N
1♦	1♠
2 NT	3 NT

West leads the five of hearts to East's queen. How should declarer plan the play?

44. Love all; dealer South. Contract: 3 NT by South.

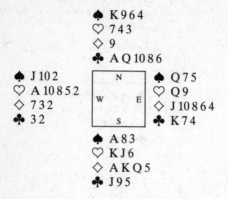

♠ K964
♡ 743
◇ 9
♣ A Q 10 8 6

♠ J 10 2
♡ A 10 8 5 2
◇ 7 3 2
♣ 3 2

♠ Q 7 5
♡ Q 9
◇ J 10 8 6 4
♣ K 7 4

♠ A 8 3
♡ K J 6
◇ A K Q 5
♣ J 9 5

The play
South should allow the ♡Q to win the first trick. No doubt East will continue the suit, but it is immaterial whether West wins the heart continuation or not, as South can now take the club finesse in safety. East can make his ♣K, but declarer is assured of 4 clubs, 2 spades, 1 heart and 3 diamonds. If South wins the first trick with the ♡K, he will be defeated – the defence will make 4 hearts and 1 club.

The principle
A vital decision in a particular suit should often be based on the distribution of another key suit. In this case declarer cannot succeed without establishing the clubs. If West holds the ♣K there is no danger, but if East holds this card he will be able to play a second heart through declarer's remaining ♡Jx – unless the communications are broken by the duck of the ♡Q on the first trick. Contrast the apparently similar hand 24, where there is a crucial difference.

45. Love all; dealer West.   Contract: 4S by South.

♠ 10 9 8
♡ J 9 4
♢ A 5 3
♣ A K J 2

```
        N
    W       E
        S
```

♠ A Q J 7 3
♡ 6 2
♢ K Q 10
♣ 10 9 6

The bidding

S	W	N	E
—	Pass	1 NT	Pass
3♠	Pass	4♠	Pass
Pass	Pass		

West leads the three top hearts (AKQ). South ruffs, enters dummy with the ace of diamonds and takes the spade finesse, losing to West's king. West exits with the four of spades. How should South continue?

45. Love all; dealer West.   Contract: 4S by South.

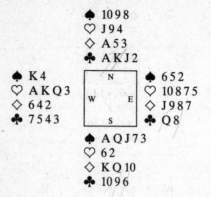

```
                  ♠ 10 9 8
                  ♡ J 9 4
                  ◇ A 5 3
                  ♣ A K J 2
    ♠ K 4                          ♠ 6 5 2
    ♡ A K Q 3                      ♡ 10 8 7 5
    ◇ 6 4 2                        ◇ J 9 8 7
    ♣ 7 5 4 3                      ♣ Q 8
                  ♠ A Q J 7 3
                  ♡ 6 2
                  ◇ K Q 10
                  ♣ 10 9 6
```

The play

Declarer should draw the last trump and cash the ♣AK, rejecting the finesse. West passed originally, yet he is known to have the ♡AKQ and ♠K; it is inconceivable that he can hold the ♣Q as well. When the ♣Q drops, declarer can count: 4 spades, 3 diamonds and 3 clubs.

The principle

When deciding how to play a critical suit, remember to go back over the bidding. Taking the bidding in conjunction with any clues from the early play, a 'guess' may become a certainty. In the above hand, the odds strongly favour a club finesse, but the bidding and play to the first five tricks make it clear that the finesse must fail. The only hope, therefore, is that East will have the singleton or doubleton queen.

46. Love all; dealer South.   Contract: 6C by South.

                    ♠ K Q 5
                    ♡ A J 10 4
                    ◇ 8 3
                    ♣ Q 5 3 2

```
              N
        W           E
              S
```

                    ♠ J 10 3
                    ♡ K Q 9
                    ◇ A J
                    ♣ A K 9 6 4

The bidding

S	N
1♣	1♡
2 NT	3♣
3♡	3♠
4 NT	5◇
6♣	

West leads the king of diamonds. How should South plan the play?

46. Love all; dealer South.   Contract: 6C by South.

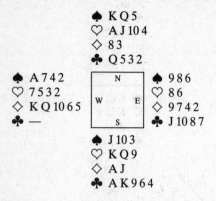

```
                    ♠ K Q 5
                    ♡ A J 10 4
                    ◇ 8 3
                    ♣ Q 5 3 2
  ♠ A 7 4 2          N          ♠ 9 8 6
  ♡ 7 5 3 2                      ♡ 8 6
  ◇ K Q 10 6 5   W       E      ◇ 9 7 4 2
  ♣ —                S           ♣ J 10 8 7
                    ♠ J 10 3
                    ♡ K Q 9
                    ◇ A J
                    ♣ A K 9 6 4
```

The play

South should win the diamond lead with his ace and play a low club to the queen. He returns a club towards the closed hand, East playing the ten (best), and wins with the ace. He overtakes the ♡9 with dummy's ten and plays a third club, enabling him to pick up all the trumps without loss. The ♡K is followed by the ♡Q which is overtaken in dummy. Dummy's ♡J provides South with a discard for his losing diamond. Having conceded a trick to the ♣A, his only loser, declarer claims the rest.

The principle

Although it is usually right to play a top honour from the hand containing two of the top three honours (as with KQ10xx opposite A9xx), this is a mistake when you are missing J10xx. In the above example, should West hold all the missing trumps, declarer is powerless, so he rightly directs his mind to the occasion when they might all be with East.

47. Love all; dealer South.   Contract: 3H by South.

                     ♠ A K 9 7
                     ♡ 8 6 4 2
                     ◇ K 7 3
                     ♣ J 2

                    ┌──────────┐
                    │   N   │
                    │ W   E │
                    │   S   │
                    └──────────┘

                     ♠ Q 6 3
                     ♡ A 7 5 3
                     ◇ 10 2
                     ♣ A Q 7 4

The bidding

          S   N
          1 NT   2♣
          2♡   3♡
          Pass

West leads the queen of diamonds, covered by the king and ace.
The defence continues diamonds, South ruffing the third round.
How should South plan the play?

47. Love all; dealer South.　　　Contract: 3H by South.

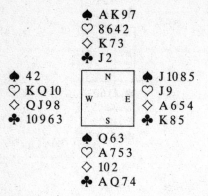

```
              ♠ A K 9 7
              ♡ 8 6 4 2
              ◇ K 7 3
              ♣ J 2
   ♠ 4 2          N          ♠ J 10 8 5
   ♡ K Q 10              W E  ♡ J 9
   ◇ Q J 9 8          S       ◇ A 6 5 4
   ♣ 10 9 6 3                 ♣ K 8 5
              ♠ Q 6 3
              ♡ A 7 5 3
              ◇ 10 2
              ♣ A Q 7 4
```

The play

To make this contract declarer will need some luck. Apart from a
3–2 trump break he also requires a successful club finesse. The
first move is a small heart from both hands. Declarer wins the
return, cashes the ♡A and plays a spade to the ace. He follows
with the club finesse. When this succeeds, declarer continues with
the ♠Q and a spade towards dummy, giving West the option of
ruffing. West should discard, but in any case dummy's losing
spade can be ruffed with South's remaining trump. South makes:
2 hearts, 3 spades, 2 clubs and 2 ruffs.

The principle

To keep trump control, consider the best time to release your big
gun(s). In the above example it would be fatal to play the ace and
another heart. It would also be fatal to play low twice. The cannon
should be fired precisely on the second round of trumps.

48. Love all; dealer West.   Contract: 4S by South.

♠ A 8 7
♡ K 6 5 3
♢ K Q
♣ 8 6 4 2

♠ K J 10 6 5 4
♡ A J 9
♢ J 10
♣ J 5

The bidding

S	W	N	E
—	1 NT	Pass	Pass
2♠	Pass	3♠	Pass
4♠	Pass	Pass	Pass

West leads the king of clubs on which East plays the ten. West continues with a club to East's ace and East returns the nine of clubs. South ruffs, draws the trumps in two rounds (the king first followed by the knave which picks up West's Qx) and plays the king of diamonds. West wins and exits with the queen of clubs. How should South continue?

Backward finesse

48. Love all; dealer West.   Contract: 4S by South.

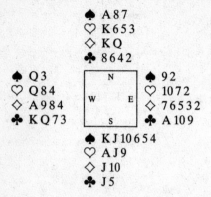

```
                    ♠ A 8 7
                    ♡ K 6 5 3
                    ◇ K Q
                    ♣ 8 6 4 2
  ♠ Q 3                          ♠ 9 2
  ♡ Q 8 4          N             ♡ 10 7 2
  ◇ A 9 8 4     W     E          ◇ 7 6 5 3 2
  ♣ K Q 7 3         S            ♣ A 10 9
                    ♠ K J 10 6 5 4
                    ♡ A J 9
                    ◇ J 10
                    ♣ J 5
```

The play

Declarer should trump the ♣Q and play the ♡J, allowing it to run
if West refuses to cover. If West plays the queen, dummy's king
takes the trick and now declarer finesses the nine on the way back.
Superficially this looks a strange play, but declarer knows that
without the ♡Q West cannot have sufficient points to justify his
opening bid. Declarer must play for the only practical
chance.

The principle

The presence of the nine in the combination AJ9 opposite Kxx(x)
affords an alternative line of play. The normal play is to lead low
towards the AJ9 and finesse the knave. However, when all the
missing points can be placed in the 'wrong' hand, as in the above
deal, then much the best chance is to start with the knave to pick
up the queen, and follow with a finesse against the ten.

49. Love all; dealer South.   Contract: 3 NT by South.

♠ 7642
♡ A82
♢ 7542
♣ 75

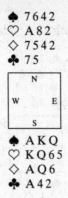

♠ A K Q
♡ K Q 6 5
♢ A Q 6
♣ A 4 2

The bidding

S	N
2♣	2♢
2 NT	3 NT

West leads the king of clubs. How should South plan the play? (If South ducks the club, West will continue top clubs until South wins.)

49. Love all; dealer South.   Contract: 3 NT by South.

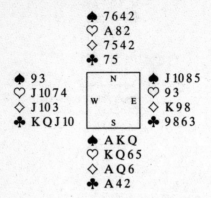

♠ 7642
♡ A 8 2
◇ 7 5 4 2
♣ 7 5

♠ 9 3
♡ J 10 7 4
◇ J 10 3
♣ K Q J 10

♠ J 10 8 5
♡ 9 3
◇ K 9 8
♣ 9 8 6 3

♠ A K Q
♡ K Q 6 5
◇ A Q 6
♣ A 4 2

The play
South has eight tricks on top and should make the most of his
three separate chances to collect the ninth, i.e. **1** the spade break;
2 the heart break; **3** the diamond finesse. Having taken the ♣A,
he begins by cashing the three top spades. When they fail to
break, he cashes the ♡KQ and ♡A – in that order. With no luck
so far he has to fall back on the diamond finesse. A small diamond
towards the AQ and, at last, he is rewarded when West can't beat
the queen. He makes 3 spades, 3 hearts, 2 diamonds and 1 club.

The principle
When you have several different chances it is important to
combine as many of them as possible so as to provide the
maximum odds in your favour. On the above hand the key is the
one entry to dummy (♡A). That is why declarer has to start with
the spades, and then play the hearts in a precise order – KQ and
then the A. Having failed to find either major suit breaking 3–3,
declarer is in the right hand to try his last chance.

50. E-W game; dealer West.　　　　Contract: 4S by South.

♠ Q 5 4
♡ 6 4 3
◇ Q 7 6 3
♣ A 10 8

♠ A K J 10 9 8
♡ Q 8
◇ K 5 4 2
♣ Q

The bidding

S	W	N	E
—	1♡	Pass	Pass
2♠	3♡	3♠	Pass
4♠	Pass	Pass	Pass

West plays the ace, king and knave of hearts, East throwing the five of clubs on the third round. How should South plan the play?

Playing for a required distribution

50. E-W game; dealer West.   Contract: 4S by South.

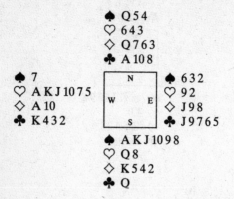

```
                    ♠ Q 5 4
                    ♡ 6 4 3
                    ♢ Q 7 6 3
                    ♣ A 10 8
    ♠ 7                          ♠ 6 3 2
    ♡ A K J 10 7 5      N        ♡ 9 2
    ♢ A 10         W       E     ♢ J 9 8
    ♣ K 4 3 2          S         ♣ J 9 7 6 5
                    ♠ A K J 10 9 8
                    ♡ Q 8
                    ♢ K 5 4 2
                    ♣ Q
```

The play
South should ruff the third round of hearts, draw trumps and play
a low diamond towards dummy. If West goes up with the ace,
South's problems are resolved. If West ducks, the queen wins,
and now a low diamond is ducked by South to West's lone ace.
Declarer makes: 6 spades, 3 diamonds and 1 club.

The principle
When you require a particular distribution to fulfil your contract,
address your mind to exploiting it, should it exist. In the above
case you must find one of your opponents with precisely ♢Ax. On
the bidding that would appear to be West. But should you decide
to place East with ♢Ax, you should play a low diamond towards
the closed hand. Then, having won with the king, you return a
diamond and duck in dummy.

51. N-S game; dealer West.   Contract: 6S by South.

♠ J852
♡ 832
◇ AKQ
♣ KJ8

♠ AKQ1096
♡ 4
◇ 1087
♣ A109

The bidding

S	W	N	E
—	3♡	Pass	Pass
4♠	Pass	5♠	Pass
6♠	Pass	Pass	Pass

West leads the king of hearts; East overtakes with the ace and returns the seven. South ruffs, draws trumps (West has two and East one) and cashes the three top diamonds (all follow). He now ruffs dummy's last heart (East throws a club). How should declarer continue?

51. N-S game; dealer West.   Contract: 6S by South.

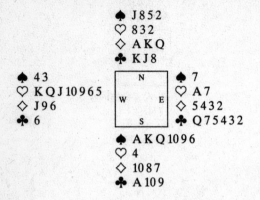

```
                    ♠ J852
                    ♡ 832
                    ◇ AKQ
                    ♣ KJ8
    ♠ 43              N           ♠ 7
    ♡ KQJ10965    W     E        ♡ A7
    ◇ J96                         ◇ 5432
    ♣ 6               S           ♣ Q75432
                    ♠ AKQ1096
                    ♡ 4
                    ◇ 1087
                    ♣ A109
```

The play
Declarer has discovered that West (the easy hand to count) started with 7 hearts, 2 spades and at least 3 diamonds – thus he cannot hold more than one club. So he cashes the ♣K, and confidently finesses East for the queen. Declarer makes: 6 spades, 3 diamonds and 3 clubs.

The principle
Counting is the most certain method of placing the cards. It is an excellent habit to acquire, although some hands are much easier to count than others. This is one of the very easy ones. You will find counting easier if you count the *original* distribution rather than attempting to reconstruct the cards that remain. Thus on the above hand West started with a 7–3–2–1 distribution, and so the club finesse becomes a certainty.

52. Game all; dealer South.   Contract: 6H by South.

♠ 64
♡ K962
♦ AQJ10
♣ A86

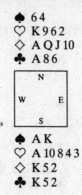

♠ AK
♡ A10843
♦ K52
♣ K52

The bidding

S	N
1♡	2♦
3NT	4♡
4♠	5♣
6♡	

West leads the queen of spades. How should South plan the play?

52. Game all; dealer South.   Contract: 6H by South.

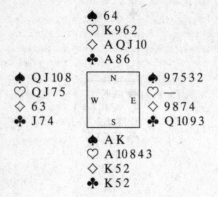

```
              ♠ 6 4
              ♡ K 9 6 2
              ♢ A Q J 10
              ♣ A 8 6
♠ Q J 10 8                    ♠ 9 7 5 3 2
♡ Q J 7 5                     ♡ —
♢ 6 3                         ♢ 9 8 7 4
♣ J 7 4                       ♣ Q 10 9 3
              ♠ A K
              ♡ A 10 8 4 3
              ♢ K 5 2
              ♣ K 5 2
```

The play

Declarer should play a low heart at trick two and, if West plays low (best), insert dummy's nine. When East shows out he can cash the ♡AK and concede a heart. Declarer's losing club goes on dummy's long diamond. He makes: 4 hearts, 2 spades, 4 diamonds and 2 clubs. As declarer has no losers outside the trump suit he must play this suit so as to lose not more than one trick, whatever the distribution. The complete safety play is to lead low from either hand and cover whatever card is played next. Provided that declarer does not play a top honour initially he can cope with all four hearts in either of the defender's hands.

The principle

When a line of play will restrict your losses to only one, and you can afford that loss, then it is advisable to pay the small premium involved (i.e. you may lose a trick unnecessarily, but you ensure that your contract is safe).

Defence

We are acutely aware of the problems that defence poses for the beginner. In these examples you will find guidance on all basic precepts, from the opening lead to simple strategy.

We plan to accompany you as you take your first tentative steps, and gently guide you through what many beginners consider at best a maze, at worst a minefield.

Contents

Standard opening leads against suit contracts
Standard opening leads against no trump contracts

Standard opening leads against suit contracts

(The best leads are usually from a high three-card honour sequence, or partner's suit.)

1 Top of honour sequence or near-sequence.
   A̲KQxx, K̲QJx, Q̲J10, J̲109x, 1̲098x, A̲Kxxx, K̲Qxx, K̲Q10x, Q̲J9x, J̲108x, A̲Kx but AK̲.

2 Fourth highest from a long suit.
   KJ74̲2, Q74̲3, J96̲4, 10863̲, Q106̲432.

3 Higher of two, except when trumps.
   96̲, 7̲4, 3̲2, K̲8, Q̲6, 10̲3, but when it is the trump suit play low: 84̲, 93̲, 74̲.

4 Top of interior sequence.
   KJ̲109, Q1̲097.

5 Highest of three small but lowest when trumps.
   96̲3, 98̲2, 6̲53, but when it is the trump suit play low: 963̲, 982̲, 653̲ (some experts advocate playing the middle trump from three small).

6 Lowest of three when headed by an honour.
   K73̲, Q104̲, J95̲, 106̲2.

7 Singleton.
   A singleton is led when it is hoped to obtain a ruff – but don't lead a singleton trump as it may damage your partner's holding.

8 Trump.
   A trump is led when you wish to cut down dummy's ruffing power. Select the normal card except with J10x̲.

Note As a general rule, do *not* underlead aces. It is seldom profitable and can be very costly. It is often wise to lead partner's suit. Indeed, he may have bid for that very purpose. Even when this turns out to be an inferior defence you can approach the post mortem with a head start! Lead a long suit when your own holding in trumps is substantial (say, K10xx) and you would like to force declarer to ruff.

Leads against slams in a suit

Although it is difficult to generalize, it is usually best to attack against a *small slam* unless partner is marked with a yarborough.

With ♠3, ♡A64, ◇9852, ♣Q10753 against 6♠ or 6♡
Lead the ♣5 if clubs have not been bid as a genuine suit.

With ♠64, ♡Q73, ◇A862, ♣8643 against 6♠
Lead the ♡3 if hearts have not been bid as a genuine suit.

With ♠K6, ♡986, ◇QJ75, ♣K1086 against 6♠
Lead the ♡9. You have too much. Partner must hold almost a yarborough, so play it safe with a negative lead.

With ♠K642. ♡—, ◇863, ♣1076432 against 6♡
Lead ♠2 if spades have not been bid as a genuine suit.

Against a *grand slam* look for a safe lead. You are not trying to develop a trick. You are trying to avoid giving one away.

With ♠J753, ♡Q8, ◇753, ♣J852 against 7◇
Lead ◇3.

A trump is often a good lead against a grand slam.

Standard opening leads against no trump contracts

(The best leads are usually from length, or partner's suit)

1 Top of honour sequence or near sequence.
   A̲KQxxx, K̲QJxx, QJ10xx, J109xxx, A̲KJxxx, K̲Q10xx, QJ9xx, J108xx.

2 Fourth highest of longest and strongest suit.
   A107̲54, KJ8̲632, Q86̲43, 107̲532, 965̲432, AK65̲3, QJ5̲42.

3 Top of interior sequence.
   AQJ̲10xx, AJ̲109x, KJ̲108x, Q10̲9xx.

4 Highest of two or three small cards.
   7̲4, 8̲6, 8̲63, 7̲42 (this lead is usually made when the bidding suggests that any alternative is unattractive – or when partner has bid the suit).

118

5 Lowest from three to an honour.

A 8 <u>3</u>, K 9 <u>6</u>, Q 10 <u>2</u>, J 7 <u>4</u>, 10 6 <u>3</u> (this lead is usually made when the bidding suggests that any alternative is unattractive – or when partner has bid the suit).

Note You will notice that underleading an ace is now completely acceptable. Partner's suit should still be given a high priority, especially if he has made an overcall.

Leads against slams in no trumps

Against *small slams* in no trumps it usually pays to make a safe lead, especially when the bidding has indicated two balanced hands.

With ♠Q74, ♡J963, ◇Q642, ♣97 against 6NT $\begin{bmatrix} 2NT-4NT \\ 6NT \end{bmatrix}$
Lead the ♣9.

With ♠10743, ♡K6, ◇875, ♣Q1064 against 6NT [1NT–6NT]
Lead the ◇8.

With ♠Q106, ♡742, ◇85, ♣A8532 against 6NT $\begin{bmatrix} 2D-2H \\ 3D-4D \\ 4NT-5D \\ 6NT \end{bmatrix}$
Lead the ♠6.

This time declarer has *not* got a balanced hand, that is why you are advised to attack with a spade lead, as you would against 6◇.

Against a *grand slam* in no trumps *always* make a safe lead.

With ♠Q1074, ♡J5, ◇J109, ♣7642 against 7NT
Lead the ◇J.

1. Love all; dealer South.   Contract: 4S by South.

♠ Q J 7 4 2
♡ A K
◇ Q 5 3
♣ J 6 3

♠ 3
♡ 9 8 6 5 2
◇ A K 7
♣ K 7 4 2

The bidding

S	N
1♠	4♠

West leads the knave of diamonds, trapping dummy's queen. As South has to follow to each round, the defence score the first three tricks, and then switch safely to a heart. Trumps are drawn in two rounds, ending in dummy, and the knave of clubs is played. How should East plan the defence?

Covering an honour

1. Love all; dealer South. Contract: 4S by South.

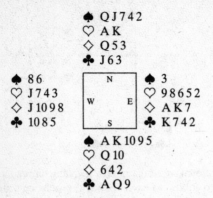

```
              ♠ Q J 7 4 2
              ♡ A K
              ◇ Q 5 3
              ♣ J 6 3
   ♠ 8 6          N          ♠ 3
   ♡ J 7 4 3                 ♡ 9 8 6 5 2
   ◇ J 10 9 8   W     E      ◇ A K 7
   ♣ 10 8 5         S        ♣ K 7 4 2
              ♠ A K 10 9 5
              ♡ Q 10
              ◇ 6 4 2
              ♣ A Q 9
```

The defence

East should cover the ♣J with the ♣K, hoping to promote a
lesser card to winning rank for his partner. Now, no matter how
declarer struggles, he will have to lose a trick to the ♣10. If East
fails to cover, declarer will bring in the club suit without loss and
the contract will succeed.

The principle

Covering an honour with an honour is a means of promoting
cards of a lower rank to winners. Usually one has to hope that
partner is the beneficiary, although sometimes one can see the
critical intermediate card in one's own hand. This is the general
rule when deciding whether to cover or not: cover if there is a
realistic chance of promoting some lower card to winning rank
for your side. Don't cover when there is not.

2. Love all; dealer South.   Contract: 3 NT by South.

♠ A K 4
♡ J 9 3
◇ J 6
♣ Q J 10 9 8

	N		♠ 7 6
W		E	♡ K Q 8 6 5
	S		◇ A 4 2
			♣ 7 3 2

The bidding

S	N
1 NT	3 NT

West leads the five of diamonds, dummy plays the knave, East the ace and South the seven. How should East plan the defence?

Returning partner's suit

2. Love all; dealer South.   Contract: 3 NT by South.

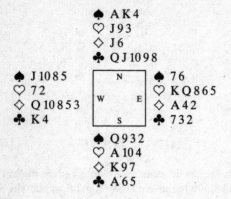

```
                    ♠ A K 4
                    ♡ J 9 3
                    ◇ J 6
                    ♣ Q J 10 9 8
        ♠ J 10 8 5      N        ♠ 7 6
        ♡ 7 2                     ♡ K Q 8 6 5
        ◇ Q 10 8 5 3  W     E    ◇ A 4 2
        ♣ K 4            S        ♣ 7 3 2
                    ♠ Q 9 3 2
                    ♡ A 10 4
                    ◇ K 9 7
                    ♣ A 6 5
```

The defence

East should return his partner's suit, playing the ◇4. West will clear the diamonds and then, when he comes in with the ♣K, cash the setting tricks. To attempt to play on hearts, for example, would be fatal.

The principle

When partner leads his suit against a no trump contract it is usually (but obviously not always) correct to continue the attack. In the above hand there is no good reason to switch, or to think that an alternative attack would be profitable.

3. Game all; dealer South.   Contract: 3 NT by South.

```
                    ♠ 62
                    ♡ Q72
                    ◇ KJ8
                    ♣ AQJ97
     ♠ A9854        ┌─────────┐
     ♡ J1086        │    N    │
     ◇ 7            │ W     E │
     ♣ 862          │    S    │
                    └─────────┘
```

The bidding

S	N
1 NT	3 NT

West leads the five of spades to East's king (5, 2, K, J). East returns the seven of spades, covered by the queen. How should West plan the defence?

3. Game all; dealer South.   Contract: 3 NT by South.

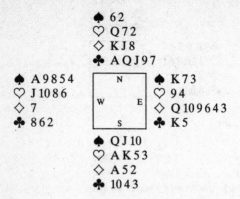

♠ 62
♡ Q 7 2
◇ K J 8
♣ A Q J 9 7

♠ A 9 8 5 4
♡ J 10 8 6
◇ 7
♣ 8 6 2

♠ K 7 3
♡ 9 4
◇ Q 10 9 6 4 3
♣ K 5

♠ Q J 10
♡ A K 5 3
◇ A 5 2
♣ 10 4 3

The defence

West should follow with the ♠4, withholding his ace. However, it would have been correct to play the ace had East returned the ♠3, marking him with a four-card suit (or possibly a doubleton). The ♠7 strongly suggests that East has three spades, and despite declarer's efforts to persuade you that he has the QJ alone, it is your partner that you should trust, not the enemy. When East regains the lead with the ♣K he will, of course, continue spades, defeating the contract by one trick.

The principle

Especially against no trump contracts, the defence must maintain its line of communication. With no outside entry a defender should preserve the high honour in his long suit so that when his partner regains the lead the link remains to cash the winners in the suit. The principle for the defender who intends to return his partner's suit is this: with an original holding of three (you are now left with two), you return the higher. With an original holding of four or more, you return the original fourth highest – unless there is a danger of blocking the suit, e.g. with AJ10x or AJ9x, return the knave.

4. Game all; dealer North.   Contract: 6S by South.

```
                    ♠ Q 10 9 6
                    ♡ A 5 4
                    ◇ J 6 4
                    ♣ K Q J
    ♠ A 5 3        ┌─────────┐
    ♡ K 10 3 2     │    N    │
    ◇ 10 9 8 7     │ W     E │
    ♣ 9 8          │    S    │
                   └─────────┘
```

The bidding

N	S
1 NT	3♠
4♣	5♣
5♡	6♠

West leads the ten of diamonds, won by South's ace. West wins
the second round of spades, East discarding a low club, and exits
with a third spade. Declarer cashes three rounds of clubs, discarding a heart, and then returns to hand with the king of diamonds
and plays the queen of diamonds, everyone following. The
queen of hearts comes next. How should West plan the defence?

Covering an honour

4. Game all; dealer North.   Contract: 6S by South.

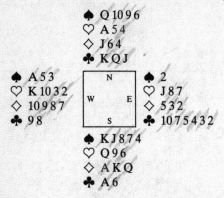

```
              ♠ Q 10 9 6
              ♡ A 5 4
              ◇ J 6 4
              ♣ K Q J
 ♠ A 5 3          N          ♠ 2
 ♡ K 10 3 2               ♡ J 8 7
 ◇ 10 9 8 7    W      E    ◇ 5 3 2
 ♣ 9 8           S          ♣ 10 7 5 4 3 2
              ♠ K J 8 7 4
              ♡ Q 9 6
              ◇ A K Q
              ♣ A 6
```

The defence

West should cover the ♡Q with the ♡K. Either South has the
♡QJ, in which case it makes no difference what West does, or
South is trying to pull a fast one and slip through the queen. By
covering the queen with the king, West frustrates South's des-
perate ruse.

The principle

It is correct to cover an honour whenever there is a realistic
chance of promoting a card held by your side. In the above
example, West could not gain by ducking. Declarer's play was
unlikely to succeed in this setting, but suppose dummy had only
two hearts and West did not have the ten:

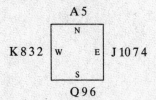

```
                A 5
                 N
        K 8 3 2  W      E  J 10 7 4
                 S
                Q 9 6
```

Now, by playing the queen, South might well steal his slam.

5. Game all; dealer North.   Contract: 4S by South.

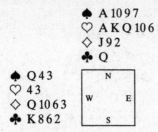

♠ A 10 9 7
♡ A K Q 10 6
♦ J 9 2
♣ Q

♠ Q 4 3
♡ 4 3
♦ Q 10 6 3
♣ K 8 6 2

The bidding

N	S
1♡	1♠
3♠	4♠

West strikes a good lead with the three of diamonds, enabling the defence to cash the first three tricks. South wins the heart switch with his knave and leads the knave of spades. How should West plan the defence, and would it make any difference if he held only two spades, Qx?

When not to cover an honour

5. Game all; dealer North. Contract: 4S by South.

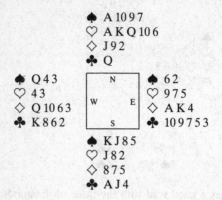

```
              ♠ A 10 9 7
              ♡ A K Q 10 6
              ◇ J 9 2
              ♣ Q
♠ Q 4 3                        ♠ 6 2
♡ 4 3           N              ♡ 9 7 5
◇ Q 10 6 3   W     E           ◇ A K 4
♣ K 8 6 2       S              ♣ 10 9 7 5 3
              ♠ K J 8 5
              ♡ J 8 2
              ◇ 8 7 5
              ♣ A J 4
```

The defence
West should play a low spade, as indeed he should if he held the
queen doubleton, or any number headed by an honour. Declarer
is obviously looking for the ♠Q. It is inconceivable that West
can promote anything for his partner by covering. In fact, if
South intends running the ♠J, his play is against the odds (the
♠K first, guarding against a low queen with East, is technically
superior play). If West plays low it is probable that declarer
intends to go up with dummy's ♠A and finesse East for the
queen. However, the psychological effort of playing the knave
first might catch an inexperienced West off guard, and declarer
can enjoy the luxury of this ploy as he holds all the intermediate
cards in the suit – except the queen.

The principle
It is a good habit to think about these situations in advance, so
that when the critical moment arrives you can follow suit at a
normal tempo. It is the height of folly to cover an honour when it
can't gain and could possibly cost.

6. Love all; dealer South.   Contract: 4S by South.

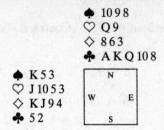

♠ 10 9 8
♡ Q 9
♦ 8 6 3
♣ A K Q 10 8

♠ K 5 3
♡ J 10 5 3
♦ K J 9 4
♣ 5 2

The bidding

S	N
1♠	2♣
2♠	3♠
4♠	

West leads the four of diamonds to East's ace (4, 3, A, 7). East returns the two of diamonds to West's king (2, Q, K, 6). How should West continue?

6. Love all; dealer South.   Contract: 4S by South.

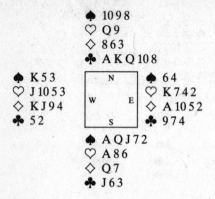

```
              ♠ 10 9 8
              ♡ Q 9
              ♢ 8 6 3
              ♣ A K Q 10 8
  ♠ K 5 3          N          ♠ 6 4
  ♡ J 10 5 3                  ♡ K 7 4 2
  ♢ K J 9 4    W       E      ♢ A 10 5 2
  ♣ 5 2             S         ♣ 9 7 4
              ♠ A Q J 7 2
              ♡ A 8 6
              ♢ Q 7
              ♣ J 6 3
```

The defence

West should switch to the ♡J. East's return of the ♢2 is highly significant; it means that he has either 4 diamonds or 2. There are two clues to suggest it is the former: **1** the ♢5 has not yet appeared; **2** with 4 diamonds headed by the Q10, South might well have preferred the rebid of two diamonds over two clubs instead of repeating his spades. The heart switch ensures that the defence will make 2 diamonds, 1 spade and 1 heart to defeat the contract by one trick. If West continues with a third diamond, declarer will have no trouble in making his contract by discarding his losing hearts on the long clubs.

The principle

Close attention to the small cards and remembering the bidding often provide a clear picture of the distribution. This enables the defence to decide whether to persevere with the same attack or to switch. On the above hand East must return the right card, the ♢2, so that West can gauge whether to attempt to cash a third diamond or not.

7. Love all; dealer South.　　　　Contract: 4S by South.

　　　　　　　　　♠ 10 9 8
　　　　　　　　　♡ A Q 4
　　　　　　　　　♢ 7 6 4
　　　　　　　　　♣ K Q J 10

```
        N        ♠ 6 4 2
                 ♡ 10 9 8 5
     W     E     ♢ Q 10 3
        S        ♣ A 6 5
```

The bidding

　　　　S　　　　N
　　　　1♠　　　2♣
　　　　2♡　　　3♠
　　　　4♠

West leads the five of diamonds. How should East plan the defence?

Third player plays high

7. Love all; dealer South.   Contract: 4S by South.

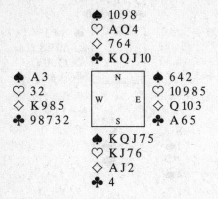

```
              ♠ 10 9 8
              ♡ A Q 4
              ♢ 7 6 4
              ♣ K Q J 10
♠ A 3                          ♠ 6 4 2
♡ 3 2          N               ♡ 10 9 8 5
♢ K 9 8 5    W   E             ♢ Q 10 3
♣ 9 8 7 3 2    S               ♣ A 6 5
              ♠ K Q J 7 5
              ♡ K J 7 6
              ♢ A J 2
              ♣ 4
```

The defence
East must contribute the ♢Q. If this is allowed to hold, East must continue diamonds. If the ♢A takes the first trick, then East must resume the diamond attack when he gains the lead with the ♣A. This defence will result in 2 diamond tricks and 2 black-suit aces: one down.

The principle
East's guideline emanates from the game of whist, 'Second player plays low, third player plays high'. There are numerous exceptions, but the principle is sound. In the above hand, declarer would fulfil his contract if East played any diamond other than the queen. Note, too, that West found the only opening lead to defeat the contract.

8. Game all; dealer South.   Contract: 2H by South.

$$\begin{array}{l} \spadesuit \text{ K J 7 5} \\ \heartsuit \text{ 8 4} \\ \diamondsuit \text{ 5 3} \\ \clubsuit \text{ A 9 6 4 3} \end{array}$$

$$\begin{array}{l} \spadesuit \text{ A 10 8 3} \\ \heartsuit \text{ J 10} \\ \diamondsuit \text{ A J 6} \\ \clubsuit \text{ J 10 8 5} \end{array}$$

```
        N
   W         E
        S
```

The bidding

S	N
1♡	1♠
2♢	2♡
Pass	

West leads the knave of hearts which is won by declarer's ace. At trick two declarer plays the six of spades. How should West plan the defence?

8. Game all; dealer South.   Contract: 2H by South.

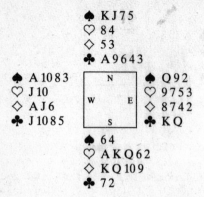

```
                    ♠ K J 7 5
                    ♡ 8 4
                    ♢ 5 3
                    ♣ A 9 6 4 3
      ♠ A 10 8 3        N         ♠ Q 9 2
      ♡ J 10                      ♡ 9 7 5 3
      ♢ A J 6     W         E     ♢ 8 7 4 2
      ♣ J 10 8 5       S          ♣ K Q
                    ♠ 6 4
                    ♡ A K Q 6 2
                    ♢ K Q 10 9
                    ♣ 7 2
```

The defence
West should play a low spade. If declarer misguesses and plays the knave the defence may well prevail. East will switch to the ♣K, and eventually his side should make 2 spades, 1 heart, 1 club and 2 diamonds. If West solves declarer's guess for him by playing the ace of spades on the first round, declarer will just get home, making 4 hearts, 1 spade, 2 diamonds and 1 club.

The principle
Although it will not always be right to duck on the first round, by doing so you will gain far more tricks than you lose. It is equally important that a defender follows suit at a normal tempo without a tell-tale pause. Develop the habit of making up your mind before declarer puts you to the test. Especially when defending against a slam!

9. E-W game; dealer South.   Contract: 4S by South.

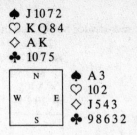

♠ J 10 7 2
♡ K Q 8 4
♢ A K
♣ 10 7 5

♠ A 3
♡ 10 2
♢ J 5 4 3
♣ 9 8 6 3 2

The bidding

S	N
1♠	4♠

West leads the king of clubs followed by the ace, and then switches to the three of hearts. Declarer wins the third trick in his own hand with the ♡A, enters dummy with a diamond and leads the ♠J. How should East plan the defence?

9. E-W game; dealer South.   Contract: 4S by South.

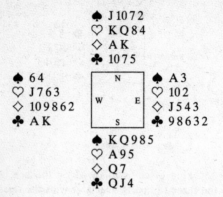

♠ J 10 7 2
♡ K Q 8 4
◇ A K
♣ 10 7 5

♠ 6 4
♡ J 7 6 3
◇ 10 9 8 6 2
♣ A K

♠ A 3
♡ 10 2
◇ J 5 4 3
♣ 9 8 6 3 2

♠ K Q 9 8 5
♡ A 9 5
◇ Q 7
♣ Q J 4

The defence
East must win the ♠J with his ace and play a club for West to
ruff. No doubt declarer would like East to think that he is
looking for the ace *and* queen of spades, but West has signalled a
doubleton club by playing the top honours in reverse order
(showing the AK alone) so East should follow his partner's
defence.

The principle
When partner starts an unambiguous defence, for example
establishing a ruff, only depart from his line if you are sure that
an alternative defence is better or at least as good.

10. Game all; dealer South.   Contract: 4H by South.

```
              ♠ Q J 9
              ♡ A 10 9 6
              ♢ A 10 9
              ♣ 5 4 2
        ┌───────────┐
        │    N      │   ♠ K 6 3
        │           │   ♡ K 3 2
        │  W     E  │   ♢ 8 6 4 2
        │           │   ♣ 8 7 3
        │    S      │
        └───────────┘
```

The bidding

S	**N**
1♡	3♡
4♡	

West leads the ace and king of clubs and follows with a third
round which South ruffs. The heart finesse loses to East, who
exits safely with a second round. The last trump is drawn and the
queen of spades played from dummy. How should East plan the
defence?

Covering an honour

10. Game all; dealer South.   Contract: 4H by South.

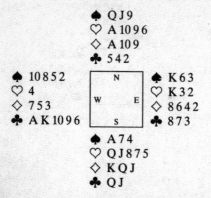

```
              ♠ Q J 9
              ♡ A 10 9 6
              ◇ A 10 9
              ♣ 5 4 2
♠ 10852          N          ♠ K 6 3
♡ 4                         ♡ K 3 2
◇ 753         W     E       ◇ 8 6 4 2
♣ A K 10 9 6     S          ♣ 8 7 3
              ♠ A 7 4
              ♡ Q J 8 7 5
              ◇ K Q J
              ♣ Q J
```

The defence

East should refuse to cover the ♠Q and wait until declarer
follows with the knave. Now it is essential to cover, in order to
promote West's ten. If East makes the mistake of covering the
first honour played from dummy, declarer will win with the ace
and lead up to dummy's J9, trapping West's ten.

The principle

When you have the choice of covering the first or second of two
equal honour cards cover the second thereby protecting your
partner's intermediates from a subsequent finesse.

The same principle applies when the suit is divided like this:

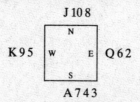

```
            J 10 8
              N
K 9 5    W         E    Q 6 2
              S
            A 7 4 3
```

When the knave is played from dummy, East must refuse to
cover. West wins with the king. Later, when declarer plays the
ten, East must cover to promote West's nine.

11. E-W game; dealer South.   Contract: 3S by South.

```
                    ♠ J9632
                    ♡ 108
                    ◇ A82
                    ♣ K53
              ┌──────────┐
              │    N     │   ♠ Q4
              │          │   ♡ 653
              │ W      E │   ◇ 9763
              │          │   ♣ A974
              │    S     │
              └──────────┘
```

The bidding

S	W	N	E
1♠	2♡	3♠	Pass
Pass	Pass		

West cashes two top hearts, declarer following with the queen
and knave. West then switches to the queen of diamonds.
Dummy wins with the ace and plays the knave of spades. How
should East plan the defence?

When not to cover an honour

11. E-W game; dealer South.   Contract: 3S by South.

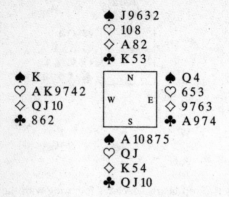

♠ J9632
♡ 108
◇ A82
♣ K53

♠ K
♡ AK9742
◇ QJ10
♣ 862

♠ Q4
♡ 653
◇ 9763
♣ A974

♠ A10875
♡ QJ
◇ K54
♣ QJ10

The defence

East must play a low spade, *not* the queen. It is inconceivable that he could promote a trick for his side by covering, so it would be pointless to do so. It would be costly, too, since declarer would then make his contract, losing 2 hearts, 1 diamond and 1 club. If East contributes a low spade, declarer must lose a trump trick as well. Nevertheless, declarer's attempted ruse is worth noting.

The principle

When deciding whether or not to cover an honour, don't forget the bidding. When there are some nine or ten cards marked between dummy and declarer, there is seldom anything to be gained by covering.

12. E-W game; dealer West.   Contract: 4H by South.

                    ♠ A J 10 4
                    ♡ Q 10 8 4
                    ◇ Q J 3
                    ♣ 8 2

                    ┌─────────┐   ♠ 8 3 2
                    │   N   │   ♡ J 5 2
                    │ W   E │   ◇ 5 4
                    │   S   │   ♣ 10 9 6 5 3
                    └─────────┘

The bidding

S	W	N	E
—	1◇	Pass	Pass
Double	Pass	2◇	Pass
2♡	Pass	3♡	Pass
4♡	Pass	Pass	Pass

West leads the ace and then the king of diamonds. How should
East plan the defence?

Petering

12. E-W game; dealer West.   Contract: 4H by South.

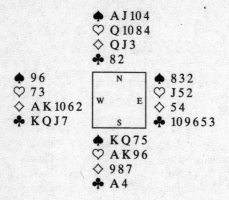

```
              ♠ A J 10 4
              ♡ Q 10 8 4
              ♢ Q J 3
              ♣ 8 2
  ♠ 9 6          N          ♠ 8 3 2
  ♡ 7 3                     ♡ J 5 2
  ♢ A K 10 6 2  W   E       ♢ 5 4
  ♣ K Q J 7        S        ♣ 10 9 6 5 3
              ♠ K Q 7 5
              ♡ A K 9 6
              ♢ 9 8 7
              ♣ A 4
```

The defence

East should play the ◇5 followed by the ◇4. This reversal of the
normal order of play, sometimes known as petering, shows an
even number of cards (in this case clearly a doubleton). West will
respond to the signal and continue with a third diamond for East
to ruff. Declarer cannot avoid losing a club to go one down.

The principle

The defence has to rely on signalling to overcome the inherent
disadvantage of not knowing its combined assets. It is normal to
play high–low with an even number of cards, low–high with an
odd number.

13. Love all; dealer South.   Contract: 4S by South.

```
                  ♠ J 10 7 4
                  ♡ A 3
                  ◇ A Q 10
                  ♣ K 6 4 3
    ♠ K 6 2      ┌─────────────┐
    ♡ J 10 9 8   │      N      │
    ◇ 8 6 2      │ W         E │
    ♣ Q 10 7     │      S      │
                 └─────────────┘
```

The bidding

S	N
1 NT	2♣
2♠	4♠

West leads the knave of hearts which declarer wins with the king, East playing the two. The ace of hearts is followed by the knave of spades which loses to West's king. How should West plan the defence?

Playing through strength

13. Love all; dealer South.   Contract: 4S by South.

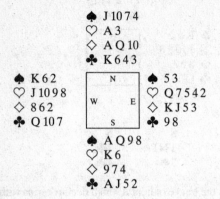

```
                    ♠ J 10 7 4
                    ♡ A 3
                    ♢ A Q 10
                    ♣ K 6 4 3
   ♠ K 6 2          ┌─────────┐      ♠ 5 3
   ♡ J 10 9 8       │    N    │      ♡ Q 7 5 4 2
   ♢ 8 6 2          │ W     E │      ♢ K J 5 3
   ♣ Q 10 7         │    S    │      ♣ 9 8
                    └─────────┘
                    ♠ A Q 9 8
                    ♡ K 6
                    ♢ 9 7 4
                    ♣ A J 5 2
```

The defence

West should play a diamond through dummy's strength. No doubt the ten will lose to the knave; East can then exit safely with a second trump, and eventually he will make his ♢K, and West will make the ♣Q for one down. If West decides to return a spade at trick four, simply opting for a passive defence, South can make his contract. Trumps are drawn and then three rounds of clubs leaves the lead with West. He can switch to a diamond but when East wins the trick he is end-played and declarer must make the remainder.

The principle

Playing through strength – especially short-suit strength – is often the best defence. There is no risk attached, and although the defence will sometimes make the tricks anyway, occasionally failure to find the switch will lead to a fatal constriction in the end-game.

14. Game all; dealer South.   Contract: 4S by South.

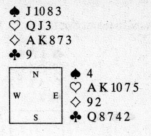

♠ J 10 8 3
♡ Q J 3
♢ A K 8 7 3
♣ 9

♠ 4
♡ A K 10 7 5
♢ 9 2
♣ Q 8 7 4 2

The bidding

S	N
1♠	4♠

West leads the four of hearts which East wins with the king (4, J, K, 6). East cashes the ace of hearts, his partner contributing the two (A, 8, 2, 3). How should East plan the defence?

14. Game all; dealer South.   Contract: 4S by South.

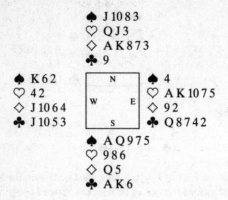

♠ J 10 8 3
♡ Q J 3
◇ A K 8 7 3
♣ 9

♠ K 6 2
♡ 4 2
◇ J 10 6 4
♣ J 10 5 3

♠ 4
♡ A K 10 7 5
◇ 9 2
♣ Q 8 7 4 2

♠ A Q 9 7 5
♡ 9 8 6
◇ Q 5
♣ A K 6

The defence
East should play a third heart, allowing his partner to make a small trump. It is obvious that West holds only two hearts, and there may not be time to wait for another lead through dummy.

The principle
When your partner starts a promising attack, consider from what holding he has initiated it. On the above hand, any other lead would have enabled declarer to get home, as a heart can be discarded on declarer's second top club. That development will surely increase partner's chagrin if you fail to give him a ruff. You should normally be able to recognize from the small cards the correct action to take.

15. Game all; dealer South.   Contract: 3 NT by South.

```
              ♠ 72
              ♡ A
              ◇ K Q J 10 9 7
              ♣ J 8 4 3
♠ 10 3            ┌─────────┐
♡ J 9 7 4 2       │    N    │
◇ A 5 2           │ W     E │
♣ 10 9 6          │    S    │
                  └─────────┘
```

The bidding

S	N
1♠	2◇
3 NT	

West leads the four of hearts, dummy's ace winning, perforce,
with East contributing the six and South the ten. The king of
diamonds is played at trick two, East playing the six and South
the four. How should West plan the defence?

Hold up

15. Game all; dealer South.   Contract: 3 NT by South.

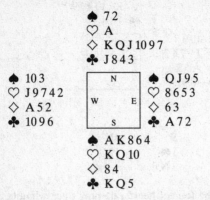

```
                    ♠ 72
                    ♡ A
                    ◇ KQJ1097
                    ♣ J843
   ♠ 103          ┌──────────┐      ♠ QJ95
   ♡ J9742        │    N     │      ♡ 8653
   ◇ A52          │ W      E │      ◇ 63
   ♣ 1096         │    S     │      ♣ A72
                  └──────────┘
                    ♠ AK864
                    ♡ KQ10
                    ◇ 84
                    ♣ KQ5
```

The defence

West should withhold his ace on the first round in an effort to cut declarer off from his diamond suit. Prospects look good because the lead struck gold, taking away dummy's entry. East's play of the ◇6 suggests that he may have a doubleton in the suit (see hand 12), but regardless of East's card, it must be right to refuse to play the ◇A immediately. No doubt declarer will play a second diamond. West will win and continue hearts. Now declarer will play on clubs, and it will be East's turn to refuse to allow him an entry to the table. If the ♣K and ♣Q are played, both rounds must be ducked. With this exact defence declarer will have to settle for 8 tricks and one down.

The principle

Aces play an important role in controlling the communications between two hands. It is up to the defence to ensure that they are properly employed. This often requires a defender to withhold an ace until the link is severed. This form of defence puts declarer in the unenviable position of owning a treasure chest but having lost the key.

16. Love all; dealer South.   Contract: 4S by South.

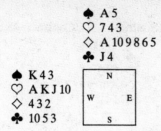

♠ A 5
♥ 7 4 3
♦ A 10 9 8 6 5
♣ J 4

♠ K 4 3
♥ A K J 10
♦ 4 3 2
♣ 10 5 3

The bidding

S	N
1♠	2♦
3♠	4♠

West wins the first two tricks with the ace and king of hearts, but the third round is ruffed by South, who now plays the queen of spades. How should West plan the defence?

When not to cover an honour

16. Love all; dealer South.   Contract: 4S by South.

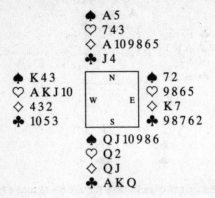

```
                  ♠ A 5
                  ♡ 7 4 3
                  ◇ A 10 9 8 6 5
                  ♣ J 4
   ♠ K 4 3          N        ♠ 7 2
   ♡ A K J 10                ♡ 9 8 6 5
   ◇ 4 3 2     W        E    ◇ K 7
   ♣ 10 5 3          S       ♣ 9 8 7 6 2
                  ♠ Q J 10 9 8 6
                  ♡ Q 2
                  ◇ Q J
                  ♣ A K Q
```

The defence
West should refuse to cover the ♠Q, ensuring one certain trump trick. If he makes the mistake of covering he will not make a trump trick at all. Subsequently declarer has to take the diamond finesse, and when this is wrong he will find himself one trick short of his contract. He loses 2 hearts, 1 spade and 1 diamond.

The principle
If by refusing to cover an honour you can make sure of a trick that you might otherwise lose, then it is right not to cover. It is as simple as that. The substance is worth more than the shadow.

17. E-W game; dealer South.   Contract: 4H by South.

$$\spadesuit \; K \, Q \, J$$
$$\heartsuit \; J \, 10 \, 8 \, 3$$
$$\diamondsuit \; K \, 3$$
$$\clubsuit \; J \, 9 \, 3 \, 2$$

$$\spadesuit \; 10 \, 9 \, 8 \, 5$$
$$\heartsuit \; A$$
$$\diamondsuit \; 5 \, 4 \, 2$$
$$\clubsuit \; A \, 10 \, 8 \, 6 \, 4$$

```
      N
  W       E
      S
```

The bidding

S	N
1♡	3♡
4♡	

West strikes a successful attack with the ace and another club.
East ruffs with the five of hearts and returns the queen of
diamonds to dummy's king. A heart is now won by West's ace,
East playing the two. West appears to be faced with something
of a dilemma. Should he play a spade so that his partner can
make the ace if he has it, bearing in mind that it might otherwise
disappear on dummy's long club, or should he give him a second
club ruff? The second club ruff, if successful, will probably result
in two down, but if East has no more trumps it may give the
contract.

17. E-W game; dealer South.   Contract: 4H by South.

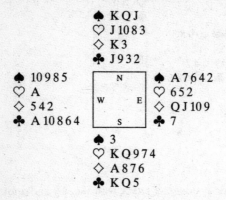

♠ K Q J
♡ J 10 8 3
◇ K 3
♣ J 9 3 2

♠ 10 9 8 5
♡ A
◇ 5 4 2
♣ A 10 8 6 4

♠ A 7 6 4 2
♡ 6 5 2
◇ Q J 10 9
♣ 7

♠ 3
♡ K Q 9 7 4
◇ A 8 7 6
♣ K Q 5

The defence
West should play a second club. By starting a peter in trumps
(the 5 first followed by the 2) East has indicated that he has a
third trump so there should be no doubt in West's mind. Having
collected four tricks East should cash the ♠A to defeat the
contract by two tricks.

The principle
A defender can tell his partner that he has three trumps by
petering (that is to say, he plays the middle card first and the
lowest one next). Note that this signal in trumps is the opposite to
signalling length in a *side* suit, where high–low means an even
number of cards. It is best to peter with three trumps only when
you want to ruff something or when it is essential to give partner
the count. However, it is invariably correct to peter with five
trumps.

18. Love all; dealer South.   Contract: 3NT by South.

```
                        ♠ 862
                        ♡ KJ5
                        ◇ 9752
                        ♣ K42
        ♠ KQ1095    ┌─────────┐
        ♡ Q104      │    N    │
        ◇ 86        │ W     E │
        ♣ 975       │    S    │
                    └─────────┘
```

The bidding

S	N
2 NT	3 NT

West leads the king of spades which is won by declarer's ace, East contributing the three. Declarer plays a low heart towards dummy, the knave holding the trick (2, 4, J, 3). The king of hearts comes next. How should West plan the defence?

Play the card you are known to hold

18. Love all; dealer South. Contract: 3 NT by South.

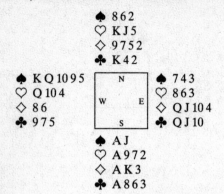

```
              ♠ 8 6 2
              ♡ K J 5
              ◇ 9 7 5 2
              ♣ K 4 2
♠ K Q 10 9 5      N       ♠ 7 4 3
♡ Q 10 4                  ♡ 8 6 3
◇ 8 6       W       E     ◇ Q J 10 4
♣ 9 7 5          S        ♣ Q J 10
              ♠ A J
              ♡ A 9 7 2
              ◇ A K 3
              ♣ A 8 6 3
```

The defence

West should play the ♡Q on the king because South knows that West holds the queen, and the queen and ten are now equals. If West follows with the ten South will know the exact position. If, however, West plays the ♡Q at trick three, declarer has to decide whether to play West for Q4 and East for 10863, or play for the drop.

The principle

When a successful finesse has marked you with a certain key card, be sure to play that card when next the suit is played, provided you have a lower card that has become promoted to the same rank. This will often leave declarer with a critical guess. Note the following:

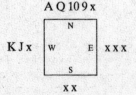

```
            A Q 10 9 x
                N
      K J x  W       E   x x x
                S
              x x
```

156

Playing in a suit contract, if declarer plays low to the queen and then cashes the ace, you must drop the king – the card you are known to hold – on the second round, leaving him unaware of the position of the knave.

19. Game all; dealer South.   Contract: 3 NT by South.

```
              ♠ A Q
              ♡ Q 7
              ◇ Q 10 7 5
              ♣ A 10 7 5 4
 ♠ 7 4          ┌─────────┐
 ♡ A J 9 6 4 2  │    N    │
 ◇ K 2          │ W     E │
 ♣ J 8 3        │    S    │
                └─────────┘
```

The bidding

S	N
1 NT	3 NT

West leads the six of hearts which is won by dummy's queen, East playing the three and South the eight. Declarer now plays the queen of diamonds from dummy. East follows with the eight, South the three and West wins with the king. How should West plan the defence?

19. Game all; dealer South.   Contract: 3 NT by South.

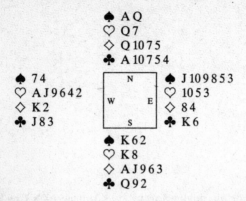

♠ A Q
♡ Q 7
◇ Q 10 7 5
♣ A 10 7 5 4

♠ 7 4
♡ A J 9 6 4 2
◇ K 2
♣ J 8 3

♠ J 10 9 8 5 3
♡ 10 5 3
◇ 8 4
♣ K 6

♠ K 6 2
♡ K 8
◇ A J 9 6 3
♣ Q 9 2

The defence

West should cash the ♡A. Partner's ♡3 on the first round is
highly significant. With a doubleton he would start a peter (play
high–low). It follows, therefore, that he must hold either the
singleton three or three cards in the suit. As there is little
prospect of defeating the contract if East holds a singleton heart,
West plays aggressively and is rewarded with a plus score of 200.
West has a further clue: from East's ◇8 it can be assumed that
South has five diamonds. If you place him with four hearts that
would make his one no trump bid on a 2–4–5–2 shape
unorthodox.

The principle

Watching partner's cards to calculate the distribution should
become a valuable habit. For his part, of course, your partner
should signal the distribution – especially in no trumps. An even
number is shown by petering (playing high–low) and an odd
number by following in natural order. In the above example,
once East has signalled correctly on the first round of hearts,
West should not go wrong.

20. Love all; dealer North.   Contract: 3 NT by South.

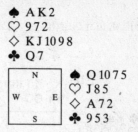

♠ A K 2
♡ 9 7 2
◇ K J 10 9 8
♣ Q 7

                    ♠ Q 10 7 5
                    ♡ J 8 5
                    ◇ A 7 2
                    ♣ 9 5 3

The bidding

N	S
1◇	1♠
2♣	3 NT

West leads the four of clubs which is won by South's ace (4, 7, 9, A). East decides to win the second round of diamonds with the ace, his partner showing a doubleton (the 5 first followed by the 4). How should East plan the defence?

Switching the attack

20. Love all; dealer North.   Contract: 3 NT by South.

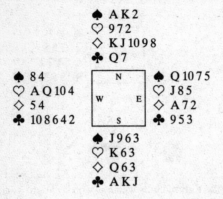

```
                    ♠ A K 2
                    ♡ 9 7 2
                    ◇ K J 10 9 8
                    ♣ Q 7
       ♠ 8 4              N              ♠ Q 10 7 5
       ♡ A Q 10 4                        ♡ J 8 5
       ◇ 5 4        W         E          ◇ A 7 2
       ♣ 10 8 6 4 2         S            ♣ 9 5 3
                    ♠ J 9 6 3
                    ♡ K 6 3
                    ◇ Q 6 3
                    ♣ A K J
```

The defence
East should switch to the ♡J. The play to the first trick makes it clear that the club suit offers no prospects for the defence. If declarer lacked the ♣KJ10 he would have risen with dummy's queen. Dummy's weakness in hearts pinpoints the switch, and the ♡J is the only card to do sufficient damage.

The principle
Especially in no trumps, when it is clear that the opening lead has failed to strike gold and that to persevere with it cannot defeat the contract, look for a weakness that can be exploited. It may also be necessary to select a particular card – as in the above example, where this is the last time East will be on lead. If East chooses a small heart, declarer can play low, restricting his heart losses to two.

21. Game all; declarer South. Contract: 4S by South.

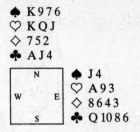

♠ K976
♡ KQJ
◇ 752
♣ AJ4

♠ J4
♡ A93
◇ 8643
♣ Q1086

The bidding

S	N
1♠	4♠

West leads the two of hearts to East's ace. How should East plan the defence?

Playing up to weakness

21. Game all; dealer South.   Contract: 4S by South.

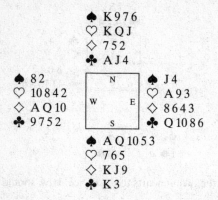

                    ♠ K 9 7 6
                    ♡ K Q J
                    ◇ 7 5 2
                    ♣ A J 4

    ♠ 8 2   N   ♠ J 4
    ♡ 10 8 4 2   ♡ A 9 3
    ◇ A Q 10   W   E   ◇ 8 6 4 3
    ♣ 9 7 5 2   S   ♣ Q 10 8 6

                    ♠ A Q 10 5 3
                    ♡ 7 6 5
                    ◇ K J 9
                    ♣ K 3

The defence

East should take the opportunity of attacking dummy's weakness
and play a diamond. West will win and exit safely with another
heart. Subsequently he will come to two more diamond tricks to
defeat the contract. If East makes the mistake of exiting pass-
ively with a heart, declarer will draw trumps, eliminate clubs and
hearts, finishing in dummy, and then play a diamond towards his
hand. West wins this trick but is now end-played, and the contract succeeds. It is important that East returns the ◇8 or ◇6 at
trick two, lest West conceives the notion that East has the king
and thinks it is imperative to cash three diamonds before
declarer can obtain a discard.

The principle

If there is nothing more obvious for the defenders to do, it is
usually right to play either through strength or up to weakness.
In the example hand, East has a golden opportunity of doing
both – playing through strength (supposed) and up to weakness
on the table. But he has a duty to play a card that will not
mislead his partner.

162

22. N-S game; dealer South.   Contract: 4H by South.

```
                    ♠ 5 4 3
                    ♡ A 9 3
                    ◇ Q 7 4
                    ♣ 8 5 4 2
        ♠ 8 7              ┌─────────┐
        ♡ K J 4           │    N    │
        ◇ 8 6 3 2       W │ W     E │ E
        ♣ J 7 6 3        │    S    │
                          └─────────┘
```

The bidding

S	W	N	E
1♡	No	2♡	2♠
4♡			

West leads the eight of spades which is won by declarer's ace (8, 3, 9, A). A small heart is now led towards the dummy. How should West plan the defence?

Don't squander your trump honours

32. N-S game; dealer South. Contract: 4H by South.

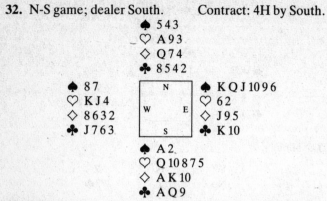

```
              ♠ 5 4 3
              ♡ A 9 3
              ◇ Q 7 4
              ♣ 8 5 4 2
  ♠ 8 7            N        ♠ K Q J 10 9 6
  ♡ K J 4                   ♡ 6 2
  ◇ 8 6 3 2     W     E     ◇ J 9 5
  ♣ J 7 6 3         S       ♣ K 10
              ♠ A 2
              ♡ Q 10 8 7 5
              ◇ A K 10
              ♣ A Q 9
```

The defence

West must play the ♡4, not the knave. Regardless of declarer's plan, it can only help him if West contributes an honour. It is quite possible that the declarer intends putting up the ♡A, in which case he will lose 2 hearts, 1 spade and 1 club. If West makes the mistake of playing the ♡J at trick two the contract will be made with the loss of only three tricks – one heart, one spade and one club.

The principle

Apart from the fact that it is usually correct for second player to play low, a defender should rarely contribute a trump honour on the first round. At best it may resolve declarer's guess, at worst it can lose a trick by force. Suppose the trump suit is distributed like this:

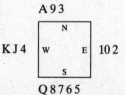

```
             A 9 3
                N
  K J 4     W     E    10 2
                S
             Q 8 7 6 5
```

Declarer, without West's assistance, cannot avoid two trump losers once he has started the suit from hand.

23. Game all; dealer South.   Contract: 3 NT by South.

```
            ♠ 62
            ♡ KQJ6
            ◇ 9642
            ♣ 853
         ┌─────────┐
         │    N    │   ♠ 1073
         │         │   ♡ 975
         │  W   E  │   ◇ A873
         │         │   ♣ Q62
         │    S    │
         └─────────┘
```

The bidding

S	N
2 NT	3♣
3◇	3 NT

West leads the five of spades which is won by South's king (5, 2, 10, K). South plays the king of diamonds, on which West throws the four of spades and East ducks. East wins the diamond continuation, on which West throws the eight of spades. How should East continue the defence?

23. Game all; dealer South.   Contract: 3 NT by South.

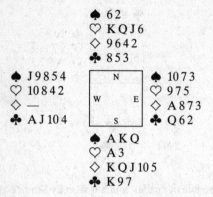

```
              ♠ 62
              ♡ KQJ6
              ◇ 9642
              ♣ 853
♠ J9854                    ♠ 1073
♡ 10842      N             ♡ 975
◇ —        W   E           ◇ A873
♣ AJ104      S             ♣ Q62
              ♠ AKQ
              ♡ A3
              ◇ KQJ105
              ♣ K97
```

The defence
East should switch to the ♣Q. West has made it blatantly clear that the spade suit must be abandoned, so the only hope for the defence is to make four tricks in clubs. By playing the ♣Q East can accomplish this. Part of the praise for a successful defence must go to West for his thoughtful discards.

The principle
West's ploy of throwing away the suit in which he had originally shown an interest is a common form of signalling between defenders. The onus is then on East to plot the new attack – choosing the suit and the right card.

24. N-S game; dealer South.   Contract: 3NT by South.

```
                    ♠ A 8 7 5
                    ♡ J 4
                    ♢ J 7 6
                    ♣ 10 8 6 3
    ♠ K 10 3        ┌─────────┐
    ♡ 10 8 6 5 3    │    N    │
    ♢ Q 9 2         │ W     E │
    ♣ 9 4           │    S    │
                    └─────────┘
```

The bidding

S	N
1♢	1♠
3 NT	

West leads the five of hearts. The knave is played from dummy, the queen from East and the ace from declarer. Declarer now plays the three of diamonds. How should West plan the defence?

Second player plays low

24. N-S game; dealer South.　　　Contract: 3 NT by South.

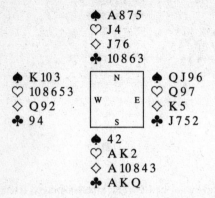

```
                ♠ A 8 7 5
                ♡ J 4
                ◇ J 7 6
                ♣ 10 8 6 3
  ♠ K 10 3       ┌─────────┐     ♠ Q J 9 6
  ♡ 10 8 6 5 3   │    N    │     ♡ Q 9 7
  ◇ Q 9 2        │ W     E │     ◇ K 5
  ♣ 9 4          │    S    │     ♣ J 7 5 2
                └─────────┘
                ♠ 4 2
                ♡ A K 2
                ◇ A 10 8 4 3
                ♣ A K Q
```

The defence

West should play low and allow his partner to win the ◇K and
return a second heart. Now declarer has no play for the contract.
If West makes the mistake of going up with the ◇Q at trick two,
declarer will make 1 spade, 2 hearts, 4 diamonds and 3 clubs.
Occasionally West's play will cost a trick, but it will show a good
profit on balance.

The principle

Although bridge players should never play by rote there is much
to be said for the old rule that emanates from the game of whist,
'Second player plays low, third player plays high'. There are
many exceptions, but in general the rule is sound.

25. Love all; dealer North.   Contract: 3 NT by South.

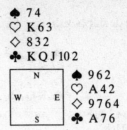

♠ 74
♡ K 6 3
◇ 8 3 2
♣ K Q J 10 2

	N		♠ 9 6 2
W		E	♡ A 4 2
			◇ 9 7 6 4
	S		♣ A 7 6

The bidding

N	S
Pass	1H
2C	3 NT

West leads the queen of spades, which is allowed to hold, East
following with the two. The spade continuation is won by the
ace, East playing the six. Declarer now plays the five of clubs to
dummy's ten, West following with the three. How should East
plan the defence? (If the ♣10 is allowed to hold, declarer
continues with the ♣K.)

25. Love all; dealer North.   Contract: 3 NT by South.

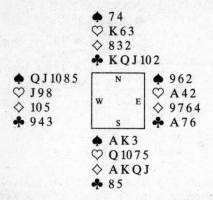

♠ 74
♡ K 6 3
◇ 8 3 2
♣ K Q J 10 2

♠ Q J 10 8 5
♡ J 9 8
◇ 10 5
♣ 9 4 3

♠ 9 6 2
♡ A 4 2
◇ 9 7 6 4
♣ A 7 6

♠ A K 3
♡ Q 10 7 5
◇ A K Q J
♣ 8 5

The defence

East should win the second round of clubs and play his last spade. When West followed to the first club with the three (the lowest card, showing an odd number) he was signalling three cards in the suit, leaving the declarer with two. If East makes the mistake of either winning the first club or ducking the second, declarer will get home. If permitted to make two clubs he will switch to hearts, as he will need only one additional trick for his contract. Having defended correctly so far, East must hold off if South subsequently plays the ♡Q from his hand, to prevent dummy gaining an entry. This accurate defence holds declarer to eight tricks.

The principle

Signals are invaluable to the defence. The above hand is an illustration of signalling distribution. The traditional method is to peter (play high–low) with an even number and follow naturally with an odd. Had West held the ♣9 3 he would have played the 9 first, and East would have held off until the third round.

26. Love all; dealer South.   Contract: 4S by South.

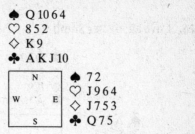

♠ Q 10 6 4
♡ 8 5 2
◇ K 9
♣ A K J 10

♠ 7 2
♡ J 9 6 4
◇ J 7 5 3
♣ Q 7 5

The bidding

S	N
1♠	4♠

West leads the king of hearts. How should East plan the defence?

26. Love all; dealer South.   Contract: 4S by South.

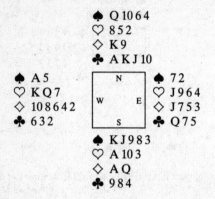

♠ Q 10 6 4
♡ 8 5 2
◇ K 9
♣ A K J 10

♠ A 5
♡ K Q 7
◇ 10 8 6 4 2
♣ 6 3 2

♠ 7 2
♡ J 9 6 4
◇ J 7 5 3
♣ Q 7 5

♠ K J 9 8 3
♡ A 10 3
◇ A Q
♣ 9 8 4

The defence
East should play the ♡9, encouraging West to continue the suit
that has set the defence off on the right lines. If East plays a low
card there is a danger that West may switch, fearing that South has
♡AJx. If West switches to a diamond, South will be careful to
conceal his ace. He will play low from dummy and cover East's
knave with the queen. When West regains the lead with the ♠A
he may try and cash his partner's ◇A! This will permit declarer to
draw trumps and take a club finesse; this will lose, but then
declarer can discard his small heart on dummy's fourth club.

The principle
One of the ways defenders can tell each other if they like or dislike
a suit is to follow with an especially high or low card. What
constitutes a high or low card depends on the particular setting,
but the 9, 8, 7 are generally regarded as high while the 2, 3, 4 are
low. A high card denotes encouragement. A low card shows lack
of interest. When encouraging, it is wise to play the highest card
you can afford, to avoid ambiguity.

27. Love all; dealer South.   Contract: 3 NT by South.

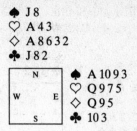

♠ J 8
♡ A 4 3
◇ A 8 6 3 2
♣ J 8 2

♠ A 10 9 3
♡ Q 9 7 5
◇ Q 9 5
♣ 10 3

The bidding

S	N
1♣	1◇
2 NT	3 NT

West leads the five of spades. How should East plan the defence?
Would it make any difference if East's spades were A1032?

Returning the right card

27. Love all; dealer South.   Contract: 3 NT by South.

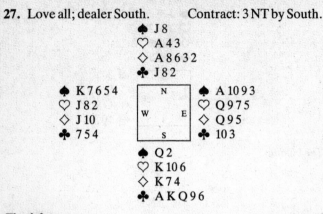

```
                        ♠ J 8
                        ♡ A 4 3
                        ◇ A 8 6 3 2
                        ♣ J 8 2
     ♠ K 7 6 5 4         N         ♠ A 10 9 3
     ♡ J 8 2                        ♡ Q 9 7 5
     ◇ J 10         W        E      ◇ Q 9 5
     ♣ 7 5 4                        ♣ 10 3
                        S
                        ♠ Q 2
                        ♡ K 10 6
                        ◇ K 7 4
                        ♣ A K Q 9 6
```

The defence

East should win the ♠A and return the ♠10. Now the defence will be able to collect all five spade winners to defeat the contract. If East sticks slavishly to the rule of returning his original fourth highest (as he would with A1032 – returning the 2), the suit will be blocked and the defence will be unable to take more than four tricks.

The principle

Normally the most helpful thing you can do is return the correct card to let partner know the distribution. If East wins with a top honour – say the ace – when holding a number of smaller cards he would return the card underlined in the following examples: A8̲2, A85̲2, A85̲3̲2. The exception is when there is a serious danger of blocking the suit with holdings like AJ103, A1094, and possibly A1083. Now the second highest card should be returned, to avoid a blockage. Even experts make mistakes in this situation. Looking at the diagram, West appears to have no problem. But an alert South who held ♠Q92 originally might follow with ♠Q to the second trick, secure in the knowledge that his ♠9 would win the third round of the suit. In a different setting West's only defence would be to duck! Bridge is not always an easy game, but that doesn't absolve East from returning the right card.

28. E-W game; dealer South.   Contract: 4H by South.

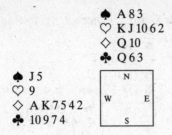

♠ A 8 3
♡ K J 10 6 2
♢ Q 10
♣ Q 6 3

♠ J 5
♡ 9
♢ A K 7 5 4 2
♣ 10 9 7 4

The bidding

	S	N
	1♡	4♡

West leads the ace and king of diamonds, East following with the three and knave, and South the six and nine. How should West continue the defence?

Don't give a ruff and discard

28. E-W game; dealer South.   Contract: 4H by South.

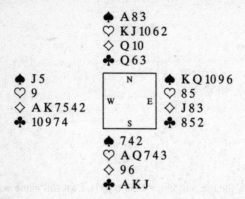

The defence

Whatever West does he must not continue diamonds. A third round would enable the declarer to ruff in one hand and discard in the other, with the effect that one of his spade losers would disappear. Superficially, perhaps the ♣10 is the most attractive switch, but West should construe East's ◇J as an invitation to switch to spades.

The principle

Defenders must be careful to avoid conceding a ruff and discard, enabling the declarer, when he has no more of the suit led in either hand, to ruff in the hand of his choice and discard in the opposite hand. It is true that there are some situations where this 'heinous crime' is in fact the only defence (see hand 29), but be sure of your ground before you deliberately concede what the Americans call a 'ruff-and-sluff'.

It should be noted that defenders with three cards in a suit can often emit a suit preference signal on the *second* round of the suit by choosing between the remaining cards. In the above case the ◇J was an unmistakable request for a spade switch. If East had a doubleton he would have played the ◇J on the first round.

29. Game all; dealer North.   Contract: 4H by South.

```
              ♠ 6 4
              ♡ K J 10
              ◇ A Q J 10 8
              ♣ A K J
         ┌───────────┐   ♠ A K 10 8 3
         │     N     │   ♡ 3
         │ W       E │   ◇ 6 5 4
         │     S     │   ♣ 7 5 3 2
         └───────────┘
```

The bidding

N	S
1◇	1♡
3♣	3◇
3♡	4♡

West leads the two of spades to East's king (2, 4, K, 7). East continues with the ace of spades, South playing the queen (A, Q, 5, 6). How should East continue?

The time to give a ruff and discard

29. Game all; dealer North.　　　　Contract: 4H by South.

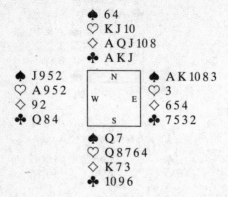

```
              ♠ 64
              ♡ K J 10
              ♢ A Q J 10 8
              ♣ A K J
  ♠ J 9 5 2        N        ♠ A K 10 8 3
  ♡ A 9 5 2                 ♡ 3
  ♢ 9 2      W       E      ♢ 6 5 4
  ♣ Q 8 4          S        ♣ 7 5 3 2
              ♠ Q 7
              ♡ Q 8 7 6 4
              ♢ K 7 3
              ♣ 10 9 6
```

The defence

East should continue with a third spade, intentionally conceding a
ruff and discard. It should be clear to East that the side suits will
provide no tricks for the defence. Therefore the best chance must
be to try to weaken the opposition's trump holding. This defence
gives the declarer an unenviable choice. If he uses one of dummy's
hearts for ruffing purposes, he must lose two trump tricks. If he
ruffs in his own hand, West will continue the force by playing a
fourth spade when he wins the ♡A.

The principle

Although it is generally costly to concede a ruff and discard, this is
one of the instances when it is the only viable defence. When the
side suits offer no prospects, the only hope is to try to bore a hole
in the opposition's trumps.

30. Love all; dealer South.   Contract: 4H by South.

```
                        ♠ A Q 4
                        ♡ 5 4
                        ◇ K Q J 10 3
                        ♣ 9 8 6
                  ┌─────────────┐
                  │      N      │  ♠ 10 9 7 5 2
                  │             │  ♡ 9 3
                  │  W       E  │  ◇ 9 8 7
                  │             │  ♣ J 4 2
                  │      S      │
                  └─────────────┘
```

The bidding

S	W	N	E
1♡	2♣	2◇	Pass
2♡	Pass	3♣	Pass
3♡	Pass	4♡	Pass
Pass	Pass		

West leads the three top clubs, South ruffing the third round. A spade is led to dummy's queen and a heart played from the table, West taking declarer's king with his ace. West now plays a fourth round of clubs. How should East continue the defence?

179

30. Love all; dealer South.   Contract: 4H by South.

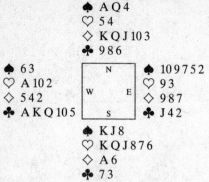

```
              ♠ A Q 4
              ♡ 5 4
              ♦ K Q J 10 3
              ♣ 9 8 6
♠ 6 3            N        ♠ 10 9 7 5 2
♡ A 10 2      W     E     ♡ 9 3
♦ 5 4 2          S        ♦ 9 8 7
♣ A K Q 10 5             ♣ J 4 2
              ♠ K J 8
              ♡ K Q J 8 7 6
              ♦ A 6
              ♣ 7 3
```

The defence

Regardless of whether dummy ruffs this trick or not, East should ruff with the ♡9 in an effort to promote an extra trump trick for his partner. This play, which is known as an uppercut, establishes the fourth trick for the defence.

The principle

By ruffing with otherwise useless trumps it may be possible to promote an extra trick for partner. Sometimes the process will have to be repeated to produce the vital trick, an uppercut and a right cross as it were. Suppose the trump suit is divided like this:

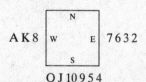

```
          N
A K 8  W     E  7 6 3 2
          S
       Q J 10 9 5 4
```

Without *two* uppercuts declarer will knock out the ace and king and draw trumps, losing just two tricks in the suit. But suppose West leads a card that his partner can ruff – East will put in the *six*, drawing South's nine. The queen and knave are required to dislodge the ace and king leaving declarer with the ten. But a further ruff by East with the seven will now promote his partner's eight.

31. Game all; dealer South.   Contract: 3S by South.

                    ♠ K 7 4 2
                    ♡ 7 4 2
                    ◇ K 5
                    ♣ Q 8 7 3

    ♠ 10 8 3   ┌─────────┐
    ♡ 5   │   N   │
    ◇ Q J 9 7 4   │ W   E │
    ♣ K 10 6 5   │   S   │
                          └─────────┘

The bidding

            S   N
            1♠   2♣
            3♡   3♠
            Pass

West leads the five of hearts to his partner's ace. East returns the three of hearts, South plays the knave and West ruffs. How should West continue the defence?

31. Game all; dealer South.   Contract: 3S by South.

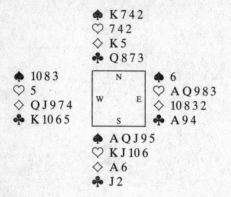

♠ K 7 4 2
♥ 7 4 2
♦ K 5
♣ Q 8 7 3

♠ 10 8 3   ♠ 6
♥ 5   ♥ A Q 9 8 3
♦ Q J 9 7 4   ♦ 10 8 3 2
♣ K 10 6 5   ♣ A 9 4

♠ A Q J 9 5
♥ K J 10 6
♦ A 6
♣ J 2

The defence

West should play a club to his partner's ace, so that he can receive a second heart ruff. The club king becomes the setting trick. Although a diamond looks a safer bet, West must trust his partner. East has returned his smallest heart, indicating a club entry. Had he held the ♦A, he would have returned the ♥9.

The principle

When the defence embark on a ruffing campaign it is good technique to indicate where the card of re-entry lies. Obviously the suit that is to be ruffed and the trump suit are ignored, leaving just the two remaining suits. If the card of re-entry lies in the higher ranking of those two – return a *high* card. But if the re-entry is in the lower ranking – return a *low* card.

32. Game all; dealer South.   Contract: 3 NT by South.

                      ♠ K 10 7
                      ♡ K 5
                      ◇ Q J 10 5 2
                      ♣ A 7 4

♠ Q 8 3   ┌─────────────┐
♡ A J 10 9 6 2   │   N   │
◇ K 3   │ W   E │
♣ 8 5   │   S   │
                     └─────────────┘

The bidding

        S   N
       1 NT   3 NT

West leads the knave of hearts which is won by dummy's king, East following with the eight and South the four. The diamond finesse loses to West's king (Q, 7, 6, K). How should West plan the defence?

32. Game all; dealer South. Contract: 3 NT by South.

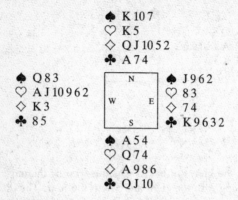

♠ K 10 7
♡ K 5
◇ Q J 10 5 2
♣ A 7 4

♠ Q 8 3
♡ A J 10 9 6 2
◇ K 3
♣ 8 5

♠ J 9 6 2
♡ 8 3
◇ 7 4
♣ K 9 6 3 2

♠ A 5 4
♡ Q 7 4
◇ A 9 8 6
♣ Q J 10

The defence

West should switch to a black suit. Clubs appear to offer better prospects than spades. It is clear from partner's ♡8 on the first round that he holds at best a doubleton, so West must not attempt to cash his hearts. If East has an entry that can be used before declarer makes nine tricks, he will play a heart through declarer's Qx with lethal effect. If West makes the mistake of cashing the ♡A at trick three, declarer will have no difficulty in making his contract.

The principle

The value of correct signalling is well illustrated on the above hand. Without East's revealing ♡8 West would have to guess whether to cash the ♡A or not. By starting a peter (playing high–low) East indicates an even number of cards in the suit, in this case clearly a doubleton. (If it is a singleton, the defence is lost.)

33. Love all; dealer South.   Contract: 4S by South.

```
              ♠ Q J 7
              ♡ 8 2
              ◇ Q 9 5
              ♣ A J 10 9 6
         ┌─────────────┐
         │      N      │  ♠ 6 3 2
         │             │  ♡ 6 5 4
         │  W       E  │  ◇ A 10 8
         │             │  ♣ K 7 5 4
         │      S      │
         └─────────────┘
```

The bidding

S	N
1♠	2♣
2♡	3♠
4♠	

West leads the two of diamonds and dummy plays the nine. How should East plan the defence?

Third hand plays middle

33. Love all; dealer South.   Contract: 4S by South.

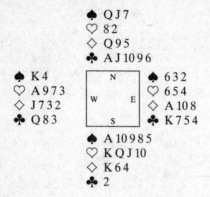

♠ Q J 7
♡ 8 2
♢ Q 9 5
♣ A J 10 9 6

♠ K 4
♡ A 9 7 3
♢ J 7 3 2
♣ Q 8 3

♠ 6 3 2
♡ 6 5 4
♢ A 10 8
♣ K 7 5 4

♠ A 10 9 8 5
♡ K Q J 10
♢ K 6 4
♣ 2

The defence

East should play the ♢10, not the ♢A. It is clear that West has led from at least one honour, the king or the knave, or conceivably from the king, knave. If it is from the king, it is unlikely that a diamond trick will disappear, so the ♢10 won't cost. If it is from the knave, East must play the ten so that the defence can cash two tricks when West gets in to lead the suit for a second time. If West holds the king, knave, it is essential for East to play the ♢10 so that the defence can take three tricks in the suit. On this hand the defence make 1 spade, 1 heart and 2 diamonds.

The principle

Although it is generally correct for third hand to play high an exception arises when a player holds a high honour accompanied by a lower honour. No firm rule is applicable, but a defender should withhold his top honour if he judges that this will enable the defence to develop extra tricks in the suit. In the above case, if East plays the ♢A on the first round the defence will make only one diamond and the contract will succeed. Note also the following lay-out:

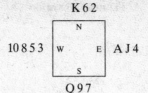

K 6 2

10 8 5 3   A J 4

Q 9 7

The three is led, dummy plays the two and East …? He must play the knave. If East makes the mistake of winning the first round with the ace, declarer has no more losers in the suit.

34. Love all; dealer North.   Contract: 3S by South.

♠ 6 5 4
♡ A K 9
♢ Q 9 3
♣ K J 9 7

♠ A 9 3
♡ 8 6 3
♢ 8 4
♣ 8 6 5 4 3

The bidding

S	W	N	E
—	—	1 NT	2♢
2♣	Pass	Pass	3♢
3♣	Pass	Pass	Pass

West leads the eight of diamonds, East winning this trick with the ten. East's ace of diamonds wins the next trick but the king of diamonds that follows is ruffed by South with the ten of spades. How should West plan the defence?

Trump promotion

34. Love all; dealer North.   Contract: 3S by South.

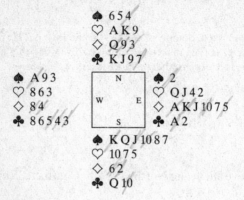

♠ 654
♥ A K 9
♦ Q 9 3
♣ K J 9 7

♠ A 9 3
♥ 8 6 3
♦ 8 4
♣ 8 6 5 4 3

♠ 2
♥ Q J 4 2
♦ A K J 10 7 5
♣ A 2

♠ K Q J 10 8 7
♥ 10 7 5
♦ 6 2
♣ Q 10

The defence

West should not be in a hurry to overruff: the ♠A won't run away, so he should discard a club. Declarer plays the ♠K at trick four and this time West wins with the ace. A club switch gives East the lead once more and a further round of diamonds seals declarer's fate. He has to ruff high and now West's ♠9 is promoted to winning rank. Had West made the mistake of overruffing the third round of diamonds, declarer would have easily made his contract.

The principle

By refusing to overruff when declarer uses a high trump, a defender can often develop an extra trick. Consider the position when the trump suit is divided like this:

75

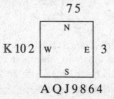

K 10 2   3

A Q J 9 8 6 4

If East is able to lead a suit in which both South and West are void, South is caught in an unenviable position; if he ruffs high, West will refuse to overruff and will make *two* trump tricks. If West makes the mistake of overruffing the knave with the king, his two remaining trumps will fall to the AQ.

35. Game all; dealer South.   Contract: 4S by South.

```
                    ♠ 9 8 7
                    ♡ A 5 4 2
                    ◇ K Q J 10 9
                    ♣ J
    ♠ K 10 4 2       ┌─────────────┐
    ♡ Q J 9 8 7      │      N      │
    ◇ 3              │  W       E  │
    ♣ K 6 4          │      S      │
                     └─────────────┘
```

The bidding

S	N
1♠	2◇
2♣	3♠
4♣	

It is West to lead. How should he plan the defence?

A forcing game

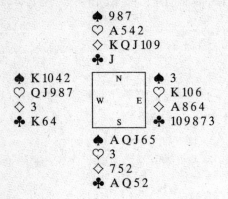

```
               ♠ 9 8 7
               ♡ A 5 4 2
               ◇ K Q J 10 9
               ♣ J
    ♠ K 10 4 2    N      ♠ 3
    ♡ Q J 9 8 7          ♡ K 10 6
    ◇ 3      W     E     ◇ A 8 6 4
    ♣ K 6 4    S        ♣ 10 9 8 7 3
               ♠ A Q J 6 5
               ♡ 3
               ◇ 7 5 2
               ♣ A Q 5 2
```

The defence

West should lead the ♡Q. Although it may be tempting to play for ruffs by leading the ◇3, this seldom pays with a trump holding as strong as West's. In fact, if West leads his singleton diamond he will obtain his ruff at trick two, but then the only other trick his side can make will be the ♠K. On a heart lead, the ♡A wins and the spade finesse loses to West. A second heart forces declarer to ruff. When declarer later loses the lead to the ◇A he is forced again, transferring trump control to West. The contract now stands no chance.

The principle

When you have a substantial holding in trumps, e.g. AJxx, K10xx, Q109x, etc., it is usually best to play a forcing game. Plug away at your long suit rather than play for ruffs. Your aim is to rest trump control from declarer, a most effective line of defence.

36. E-W game; dealer South.   Contract: 4S by South.

```
                    ♠ K 9 5 2
                    ♡ 6 2
                    ◇ K J 10 5
                    ♣ Q 8 5
  ♠ J 7 4        ┌─────────────┐
  ♡ 8 7 5 4      │      N      │
  ◇ Q 8 7 4 3    │ W         E │
  ♣ 3            │      S      │
                 └─────────────┘
```

The bidding

S	W	N	E
1♣	Pass	1◇	1♡
1♠	Pass	2♠	Pass
4♠			

West leads the three of clubs which is won by dummy's queen, East contributing the four. A small spade is played to East's ace, West following with the seven. East now plays the two of clubs, which West ruffs with the four of spades (the peter in trumps shows three). How should West continue the defence?

191

36. E-W game; dealer South.   Contract: 4S by South.

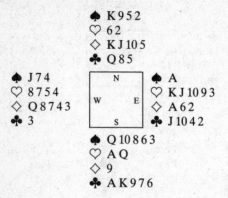

The defence

Despite East's overcall of one heart, his low card (♣2) must be respected. West should return a small diamond. East wins with the ace and returns another club for the second ruff and the setting trick.

The principle

When the defenders attempt to defeat a contract by scoring ruffs, the player giving the ruff often needs to signal where his re-entry lies. This is done by returning either a high or a low card; a high card for the higher suit, a low card for the lower suit, ignoring the trump suit and the suit in which the ruff is required. In the above example, with spades as trumps and clubs the suit that is to be ruffed, the defenders must direct their minds solely to hearts and diamonds. Had East held the ♡A, instead of the ◇A, he would have returned the ♣J at trick three.

37. Love all; dealer North.   Contract: 6S by South.

                         ♠ Q 9 7 4
                         ♡ A K 6 3
                         ◇ A 7 4
                         ♣ J 3

                                    ♠ 3
                                    ♡ J 10 7 4
                                    ◇ 9 8 5
                                    ♣ K 9 7 5 4

The bidding

          N   S
          1 NT   3♠
          4◇   5♣
          5♡   6♠

West leads the king of diamonds which is allowed to hold (K, 4, 5, 2). The queen of diamonds is won in dummy (Q, A, 8, 3). Now comes an avalanche of spades, six in fact, West parting with the ◇10, ♡2, ♡8 and ♣8, while dummy lets go the ♣J and ◇7. Which suit must East keep guarded at all cost?

193

37. Love all; dealer North.   Contract: 6S by South.

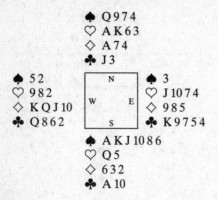

♠ Q 9 7 4
♡ A K 6 3
◇ A 7 4
♣ J 3

♠ 5 2
♡ 9 8 2
◇ K Q J 10
♣ Q 8 6 2

♠ 3
♡ J 10 7 4
◇ 9 8 5
♣ K 9 7 5 4

♠ A K J 10 8 6
♡ Q 5
◇ 6 3 2
♣ A 10

The defence

East must keep the heart suit guarded. With four hearts in
dummy, it is very likely that East alone controls the run of the suit.
West's discards confirm this, but even without that assistance East
should retain the same number of hearts as dummy. If East makes
the mistake of letting even one heart go the declarer will succeed
in making 6 spades, 4 hearts and the 2 minor suit aces, totalling 12
tricks.

The principle

When a defender holds length in a particular suit equal to that
held by dummy, it is often vital to keep the suit intact. This
especially applies where one discard either makes the suit good or
enables declarer to set it up by ruffing or ducking one round. In
the above example it is superficially tempting to place a value on
the ♣K. A moment's reflection would reveal that, unless West
has the ♣Q, the ♣K is useless and if West has the ♣Q he can be
trusted to guard that suit. Only East can guard the hearts.

38. Game all; dealer South.   Contract: 3S by South.

```
              ♠ J753
              ♡ J10
              ◇ QJ9
              ♣ AQ32
         ┌──────────┐  ♠ 10
         │ N        │  ♡ A642
         │ W      E │  ◇ 108753
         │        S │  ♣ KJ6
         └──────────┘
```

The bidding

S	N
1♠	3♠
Pass	

West leads the king of diamonds (K, 9, 3, 2) followed by the ace, on which East plays the ten (A, J, 10, 4), and then switches to the three of hearts. How should East plan the defence?

38. Game all; dealer South. Contract: 3S by South.

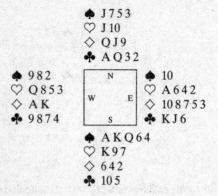

```
              ♠ J 7 5 3
              ♡ J 10
              ◇ Q J 9
              ♣ A Q 3 2
  ♠ 9 8 2        N        ♠ 10
  ♡ Q 8 5 3               ♡ A 6 4 2
  ◇ A K      W     E      ◇ 10 8 7 5 3
  ♣ 9 8 7 4      S        ♣ K J 6
              ♠ A K Q 6 4
              ♡ K 9 7
              ◇ 6 4 2
              ♣ 10 5
```

The defence
East should win the third trick with the ♡A and give his partner a diamond ruff. As West has cashed his diamond tricks in reverse order to the normal method (except with AK alone in the suit, the ace is played first), he is showing precisely a doubleton. Luckily he has found East with a quick entry, and the ruff will be just enough to defeat the contract. The ♣K cannot disappear.

The principle
When your partner seeks a ruff, do not disappoint him without good reason. On the above hand West has signalled a doubleton diamond and is obviously trying to gain entry to your hand so that he can score a ruff. East should take note of his partner's cards and ensure maximum co-operation, firstly by following to trick two with ◇10 (McKenney, asking for a heart switch; see hands 31 and 36), and secondly by giving his partner a ruff.

39. Game all; dealer South.   Contract: 3 NT by South.

♠ A 8 3
♥ K Q 10 7
♦ 6 3
♣ A 6 5 2

```
        N        ♠ Q 10 2
                 ♡ A 9 4
    W       E    ◇ J 10 8 5 2
        S        ♣ Q 10
```

The bidding

S	N
1 NT	2♣
2◇	3 NT

West leads the four of spades, East's queen winning the first trick. East continues with the ten of spades which declarer wins with the king. The three of hearts is now led to dummy's king, West contributing the two. How should East plan the defence?

Giving a guess

39. Game all; dealer South.   Contract: 3 NT by South.

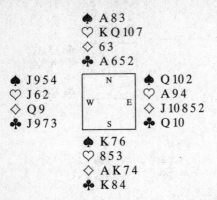

```
            ♠ A 8 3
            ♡ K Q 10 7
            ◇ 6 3
            ♣ A 6 5 2
♠ J 9 5 4               ♠ Q 10 2
♡ J 6 2                 ♡ A 9 4
◇ Q 9                   ◇ J 10 8 5 2
♣ J 9 7 3              ♣ Q 10
            ♠ K 7 6
            ♡ 8 5 3
            ◇ A K 7 4
            ♣ K 8 4
```

The defence
East should duck the ♡K – smoothly. Probably declarer will return to his hand and play a second heart. West plays small and declarer must guess correctly. Conceivably West could hold Axx and duck twice, that would be his best play. If East takes his ace on the first round, West's knave is sure to be captured on the second round.

The principle
Don't help declarer if you can avoid it, and that can mean not releasing high cards prematurely. This is how the problem appears from declarer's seat:

```
                 K Q 10 x
A x x or J x x   W         E   A x x or J x x
                 x x x
```

The early play of the ace makes declarer's task simple.

40. Love all; dealer South.   Contract: 4S by South.

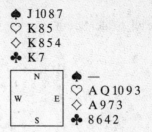

♠ J 10 8 7
♡ K 8 5
♢ K 8 5 4
♣ K 7

♠ —
♡ A Q 10 9 3
♢ A 9 7 3
♣ 8 6 4 2

The bidding

S	N
1♠	3♠
4♠	

West leads the queen of clubs, which is won in dummy with the king. When the knave of spades is played at trick two, East has to consider his discard. How should he plan the defence?

40. Love all; dealer South.   Contract: 4S by South.

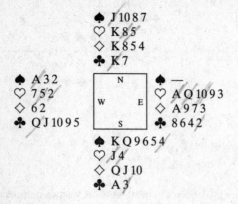

```
                    ♠ J1087
                    ♡ K85
                    ♢ K854
                    ♣ K7
    ♠ A32        ┌─────────┐      ♠ —
    ♡ 752        │    N    │      ♡ AQ1093
    ♢ 62         │ W     E │      ♢ A973
    ♣ QJ1095     │    S    │      ♣ 8642
                 └─────────┘
                    ♠ KQ9654
                    ♡ J4
                    ♢ QJ10
                    ♣ A3
```

The defence

East should discard the ♡10, the highest card he can afford in the suit he wants led. This signal is unequivocal. Without guidance, West would have a problem and might easily come to the wrong decision. If West fails to play a heart when in with the ♠A, the contract will certainly succeed. The heart switch, however, will enable the defence to score 2 hearts, 1 spade and 1 diamond.

The principle

When you can direct the defence unambiguously, especially when partner may be in the dark, do so. Normally a high discard means that you would like the suit led, whereas a low discard indicates a lack of interest. When discarding a high card, it is usual to choose the highest you can afford. Thus with AJ1098 you would throw the knave; from AQJ109 the queen would be correct.

41. E-W game; dealer North.   Contract: 4H by South.

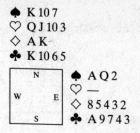

♠ K 10 7
♡ Q J 10 3
◇ A K
♣ K 10 6 5

```
        N          ♠ A Q 2
                   ♡ —
  W         E      ◇ 8 5 4 3 2
        S          ♣ A 9 7 4 3
```

The bidding

S	N
1♡	1♣
4♡	3♡

West leads the ten of diamonds to dummy's king, East following with the two. Declarer now plays the queen of hearts. How should East plan the defence?

The inferential signal

41. E-W game; dealer North.　　　Contract: 4H by South.

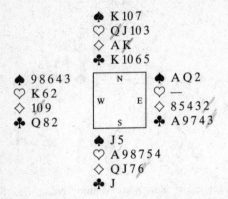

```
                    ♠ K 10 7
                    ♡ Q J 10 3
                    ♢ A K
                    ♣ K 10 6 5
  ♠ 9 8 6 4 3                       ♠ A Q 2
  ♡ K 6 2          ┌─────────┐      ♡ —
  ♢ 10 9           │ W   N  E│      ♢ 8 5 4 3 2
  ♣ Q 8 2          │      S  │      ♣ A 9 7 4 3
                   └─────────┘
                    ♠ J 5
                    ♡ A 9 8 7 5 4
                    ♢ Q J 7 6
                    ♣ J
```

The defence
Lacking a high spade that he can spare, East should discard the
♣3, displaying no interest in that suit. As East has shown no
enthusiasm in two suits (the minors) and is void in hearts, West
should take the hint and switch to a spade. This defence will defeat
the contract by one trick. If West misinterprets the message and
plays anything but a spade, declarer will be able to discard two
spades from dummy on the ♢QJ, losing only 1 spade, 1 club and 1
heart.

The principle
When you are unable to discard a high card in the suit you want
led, (a) because you have not got one, or (b) because you cannot
afford one, you can sometimes convey your message by discarding
a low card in another suit. A watchful and alert partner will
usually be able to discern the negative inference as easily as the
more positive approach.

42. E-W game; dealer South.   Contract: 5D by South.

♠ 52
♡ A Q 10 5
♢ K 8 6 2
♣ A 8 5

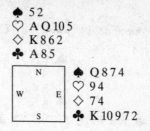

♠ Q 8 7 4
♡ 9 4
♢ 7 4
♣ K 10 9 7 2

The bidding

S	W	N	E
1♢	1♠	2♣	3♠
Pass	Pass	4♢	Pass
5♢	Pass	Pass	Pass

West leads the ace and king of spades and then switches to the three of diamonds. The declarer wins this trick and cashes five more trump winners, leaving East to find four discards. Which five cards should he retain?

42. E-W game; dealer South.   Contract: 5D by South.

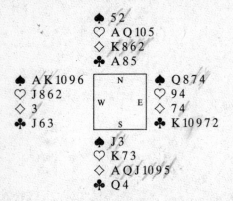

The defence
Superficially East has no problem. The two remaining spades, the two little hearts and three clubs are all expendable. However, it would be extremely foolish to part with even one small heart, because that would expose partner to a marked finesse against his knave (a heart to the ace and one back to the king and the cat is out of the bag). In fact East should part with one spade and three clubs, or two spades and two clubs. Perhaps the declarer will still get the heart suit right, but at least he will not have had it handed to him on a platter.

The principle
Although you must obviously protect the suits in which you hold high cards, you must also trry to discard in such a way that partner's holding does not become exposed. For this reason, it is sometimes necessary to resort to camouflage, as in the actual lay-out.

43. Game all; dealer South.   Contract: 3 NT by South.

```
                    ♠ A 8 6 5
                    ♡ Q 3
                    ◇ J 2
                    ♣ Q 10 9 6 2
    ♠ K 10 9      ┌─────────┐
    ♡ 7 6         │    N    │
    ◇ Q 9 7 5 4   │ W     E │
    ♣ K 8 7       │    S    │
                  └─────────┘
```

The bidding

S	N
1♡	1♠
2 NT	3 NT

West leads the five of diamonds, dummy plays the two, East the king and South the ace. Declarer cashes the ace of clubs (A, 7, 2, 5) and plays the four of clubs towards dummy. How should West plan the defence?

Giving a guess

43. Game all; dealer South.   Contract: 3 NT by South.

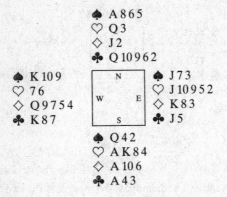

```
              ♠ A 8 6 5
              ♡ Q 3
              ◇ J 2
              ♣ Q 10 9 6 2
  ♠ K 10 9      N      ♠ J 7 3
  ♡ 7 6                ♡ J 10 9 5 2
  ◇ Q 9 7 5 4  W   E   ◇ K 8 3
  ♣ K 8 7        S     ♣ J 5
              ♠ Q 4 2
              ♡ A K 8 4
              ◇ A 10 6
              ♣ A 4 3
```

The defence
West should follow with the ♣8. The ♣J is missing, and if East has it – as is likely – declarer may misguess, playing the nine from dummy. If he does, he will be unable to recover. If West makes the mistake of going up with his ♣K, the defence will collapse and declarer will make at least ten tricks. The only excuse for taking the ♣K is the illusion that the diamonds are established. But declarer's failure to play the ◇J at trick one suggests he has A10x.

The principle
Where it is obvious that declarer has to guess the distribution of the honours in a suit, don't play your top honour unless you wish to gain the lead urgently.

44. Game all; dealer South.   Contract: 3 NT by South.

♠ Q 6 3
♡ A K
♢ 7 5
♣ A J 10 9 5 2

♠ 7 4 2
♡ J 8 6 4
♢ A 6 2
♣ K 6 3

The bidding

S	N
1 NT	3 NT

West leads the knave of spades which is taken by declarer's king. Declarer now plays the queen of clubs, losing to East's king. How should East plan the defence?

44. Game all; dealer South.   Contract: 3 NT by South.

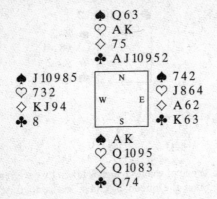

```
            ♠ Q 6 3
            ♡ A K
            ◇ 7 5
            ♣ A J 10 9 5 2
♠ J 10 9 8 5                   ♠ 7 4 2
♡ 7 3 2        N              ♡ J 8 6 4
◇ K J 9 4   W     E           ◇ A 6 2
♣ 8            S              ♣ K 6 3
            ♠ A K
            ♡ Q 10 9 5
            ◇ Q 10 8 3
            ♣ Q 7 4
```

The defence

It should be obvious to East that declarer has plenty of tricks if the defence continues along pedestrian lines. He can see 5 clubs, at least 2 hearts, 1 spade in the bag and at least one more spade to come. In different circumstances it might be right to return partner's suit, but here something more dynamic is required. The only hope lies in the diamond suit, and the ◇2 is the right card to play. This will enable West to return the suit to East's ace for a second lead through declarer. To defeat the contract the defence must take all four diamond tricks.

The principle

A defender should keep check on declarer's tricks in the same way as he keeps count of his own. Sometimes it is easy to see that perseverance with the initial attack will not defeat the contract. This is the time to consider if an alternative plan might succeed. Even if this means placing partner with exact cards, it is better to make that assumption than to capitulate without a struggle. In the above hand East needs his partner to hold good diamonds, KJ9x or KQ9x.

45. Game all; dealer South.   Contract: 6S by South.

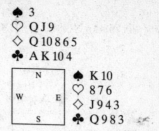

♠ 3
♥ Q J 9
♦ Q 10 8 6 5
♣ A K 10 4

♠ K 10
♥ 8 7 6
♦ J 9 4 3
♣ Q 9 8 3

The bidding

S	N
2♠	3♦
3♠	4♣
4♥	4 NT
5♠	6♣

West leads the five of clubs which is won by the ace (5, A, 9, 2).
Dummy now leads the three of spades. How should East plan
the defence?

45. Game all; dealer South.   Contract: 6S by South.

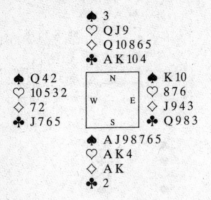

The defence

Contrary to the 'rule', second player plays low, and the advice given on hand 24, East should play the ♠K. The critical points here are the singleton spade in dummy and the second honour card in East's hand. If declarer's spades are headed by the AQJ, it won't matter which card East plays, but if the ♠Q is missing – as in the present case – declarer will take East's ♠K with the ♠A and will then have to guess which spade to play next, ♠J or ♠9. If East contributes the ♠10 on the first round South will cover with the ♠J and West will win the trick. But subsequently the ♠K will fall under the ace and the slam will certainly succeed.

The principle

When you can see that an orthodox defence is unlikely to cause declarer any problems, this is the time to create a diversion. Here is a further example:

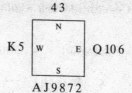

K 5   Q 10 6

A J 9 8 7 2

With plenty of entries to dummy, declarer plays a low card from the table. If East plays low, South will put in the nine, which will lose to West's king. Subsequently dummy is re-entered for a further trump lead, and now the ten will be covered by the knave, and the ace will drop the queen. If, however, East plays the queen on the first round South can win this trick but will then have to guess how to continue. Should he play East for KQx or Q10x?

46. E-W game; dealer South.   Contract: 3 NT by South.

♠ Q 7 6 4
♥ 9 2
♦ A K 8 3
♣ K Q J

         ♠ 10 5 3
         ♥ K 7 5
         ♦ 10 9 5
         ♣ 9 8 4 3

The bidding

S	N
1 NT	2♣
2♦	3 NT

West leads the knave of hearts. How should East plan the defence?

Covering partner's honour

46. E-W game; dealer South.   Contract: 3 NT by South.

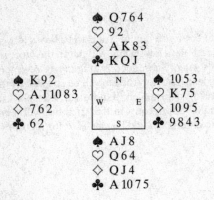

```
              ♠ Q764
              ♡ 92
              ◇ AK83
              ♣ KQJ
♠ K92           N           ♠ 1053
♡ AJ1083                    ♡ K75
◇ 762       W       E       ◇ 1095
♣ 62            S           ♣ 9843
              ♠ AJ8
              ♡ Q64
              ◇ QJ4
              ♣ A1075
```

The defence
East should play the ♡K on the first trick, lest his partner has led
from the AJ10. When the ♡K holds, East should continue with
the ♡7. If West's lead was from the J108, without the ace, East's
king would be dead anyway, sitting under the AQ, so it would
cost East nothing to contribute the king immediately.

The principle
When partner plays an honour card that could be the top of an
interior sequence, you should not finesse against him by withholding a higher honour. In the above example, if East fails to
play the ♡K at trick one, the declarer will win with the ♡Q and
make at least ten tricks.

47. Game all; dealer South.   Contract: 6H by South.

                    ♠ A 9 3
                    ♡ Q 8 6 3
                    ◇ 10 6
                    ♣ K 8 5 2

    ♠ K Q J 8 4   ┌─────────┐
    ♡ 7 4   │   N   │
    ◇ Q 9 5 4   │ W   E │
    ♣ J 4   │   S   │
                        └─────────┘

The bidding

            S   N
            2♡   3♡
            4♣   4♠
            5◇   5♡
            6♡

West leads the king of spades which is allowed to hold the trick,
partner following with the two (K, 3, 2, 5). He continues with the
queen of spades which this time dummy wins with the ace (Q, A,
6, 7). Declarer then draws trumps in two rounds, East throwing
the two of diamonds, cashes the ace and king of diamonds and
continues with another four rounds of trumps, throwing two
small clubs from dummy. Each player is now down to three
cards. Which three cards should West have retained?

47. Game all; dealer South.   Contract: 6H by South.

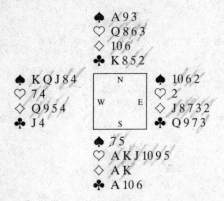

♠ A 9 3
♡ Q 8 6 3
♢ 10 6
♣ K 8 5 2

♠ K Q J 8 4
♡ 7 4
♢ Q 9 5 4
♣ J 4

♠ 10 6 2
♡ 2
♢ J 8 7 3 2
♣ Q 9 7 3

♠ 7 5
♡ A K J 10 9 5
♢ A K
♣ A 10 6

The defence

West should have retained the ♣J4 and the ♠J. The ♠J is needed as the ♠9 is still in dummy and East will have to part with his ♠10 in order to look after the clubs. But West's knave and four of clubs are also vital, to protect partner's ♣Q against a finesse. Note that the ♢Q is expendable, because if declarer had had a losing diamond he would have ruffed it in dummy before drawing all the trumps.

The principle

When discarding in the end-game a defender has two urgent tasks to perform: **1** he must protect the suits in which he has a vital holding; **2** he must assist partner to avoid declarer's snares. In the above hand the ♠J stands guard over dummy's nine, while the ♣J4 make it impossible for declarer to pick up East's queen. If West throws the ♣4, the ♣J will fall under the king, and now the A10 will form a tenace position over East's queen. If West, because he knows East has the ♠10, mistakenly keeps the ♢Q and the ♣J4, he exposes East to a squeeze in the black suits.

48. E-W game; dealer South.   Contract: 3 NT by South.

```
              ♠ A Q 8 6
              ♡ 7 5
              ◇ A Q J
              ♣ Q 10 8 4
            ┌─────────┐   ♠ K 9 2
            │    N    │   ♡ J 6 2
            │ W     E │   ◇ 10 9 7 4 3
            │    S    │   ♣ 6 3
            └─────────┘
```

The bidding

S	N
1 NT	2♣
2◇	3 NT

West leads the king of hearts. How should East plan the defence?

Avoiding a Bath Coup

48. E-W game; dealer South.   Contract: 3 NT by South.

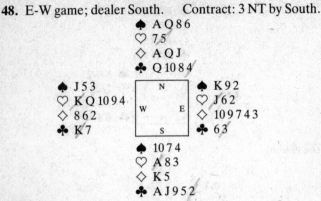

```
                    ♠ A Q 8 6
                    ♡ 7 5
                    ◇ A Q J
                    ♣ Q 10 8 4
        ♠ J 5 3           N            ♠ K 9 2
        ♡ K Q 10 9 4                   ♡ J 6 2
        ◇ 8 6 2      W         E       ◇ 10 9 7 4 3
        ♣ K 7             S            ♣ 6 3
                    ♠ 10 7 4
                    ♡ A 8 3
                    ◇ K 5
                    ♣ A J 9 5 2
```

The defence
East must contribute the ♡J to the first trick. If he fails to do so,
West will assume that South is holding off with AJx (Bath
Coup). Reluctant to lose a trick unnecessarily, he may switch
and lose an all-important tempo.

The principle
When partner leads the king against a no trump contract, it is
correct to contribute the knave if you hold it. The only exceptions are when the opening lead appears to be from a short suit,
or when dummy's holding is such that, by wasting your knave,
dummy's intermediate cards may become established. This is the
lay-out known as the Bath Coup:

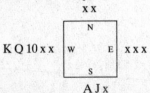

```
                    x x
                     N
     K Q 10 x x   W      E   x x x
                     S
                    A J x
```

When the king is led, South can duck, and West is faced with the
unenviable choice between continuing the suit, thereby conceding an unnecessary trick, and switching to another suit, perhaps forfeiting a valuable tempo.

49. Love all; dealer South.   Contract: 4H by South.

```
              ♠ Q 5
              ♡ 9 7 4 3
              ◇ K Q 5
              ♣ A Q 6 2
         ┌───────────┐   ♠ J 8 4
         │     N     │   ♡ Q J 5
         │ W       E │   ◇ 7 6 3 2
         │     S     │   ♣ K 8 7
         └───────────┘
```

The bidding

S	W	N	E
1♡	1♠	4♡	Pass
Pass	Pass		

West cashes the ace and king of spades and switches to the knave
of diamonds, which is won on the table. The three of hearts is
now led from dummy. How should East plan the defence?

Don't squander your trump honours

49. Love all; dealer South.   Contract: 4H by South.

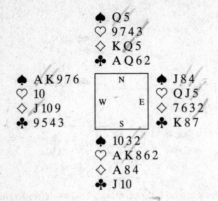

```
                    ♠ Q 5
                    ♡ 9 7 4 3
                    ◇ K Q 5
                    ♣ A Q 6 2
   ♠ A K 9 7 6    ┌─────────┐   ♠ J 8 4
   ♡ 10          │   N     │   ♡ Q J 5
   ◇ J 10 9      │ W     E │   ◇ 7 6 3 2
   ♣ 9 5 4 3     │   S     │   ♣ K 8 7
                  └─────────┘
                    ♠ 10 3 2
                    ♡ A K 8 6 2
                    ◇ A 8 4
                    ♣ J 10
```

The defence

The five is the *only* card to play. On no account should East play an honour. In this particular instance West holds the ♡10, therefore a low card from East will ensure defeat (2 spades, 1 heart and 1 club), but even if West's heart holding is totally insignificant – a void or a small singleton – declarer will surely play a top honour on the first round and only then make a decision as to the best continuation. If East makes the mistake of playing a heart honour on the first round, declarer may decide to return to dummy and finesse East for the outstanding honour.

The principle

Apart from the general 'rule' of second player plays low, it is always a good idea to try to put yourself in declarer's position. In the above case, with probably nine or ten trumps between the combined hands, it would be an unlikely line of play to finesse on the first round. And even if this is South's intention, nothing can be gained by going up with the queen or knave.

50 E-W game; dealer East.   Contract: 4H by South.

> ♠ K 10
> ♡ 10 9 7 5
> ◇ K 10 4
> ♣ Q 5 3 2

```
        N        ♠ 8 7 4 2
                 ♡ A
  W        E     ◇ 8 6 5
        S        ♣ A K J 7 4
```

The bidding

S	W	N	E
—	—	—	1♣
2♡	Pass	3♡	Pass
4♡	Pass	Pass	Pass

West leads the ten of clubs which is allowed to win (10, 2, 7, 6).
The club continuation is ruffed by South (9, 3, J, ♡4) and a heart
is played to East's ace. How should East plan the defence?

Passive defence

50. E-W game; dealer East.   Contract: 4H by South.

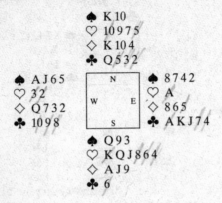

```
              ♠ K 10
              ♡ 10 9 7 5
              ◇ K 10 4
              ♣ Q 5 3 2
  ♠ A J 6 5                  ♠ 8 7 4 2
  ♡ 3 2          N           ♡ A
  ◇ Q 7 3 2   W     E        ◇ 8 6 5
  ♣ 10 9 8       S           ♣ A K J 7 4
              ♠ Q 9 3
              ♡ K Q J 8 6 4
              ◇ A J 9
              ♣ 6
```

The defence
East should continue with a top club. Many players find it difficult to persevere with a suit when they know that they will lose the lead. Nevertheless, this passive approach is often best, especially when it is obvious that there is no urgency to seek tricks elsewhere. Left to himself, declarer may well go one down if he fails to find the ◇Q. Playing West for the ♠J would also suffice but this is an unlikely line. West must play his part by following low when declarer leads a spade towards the K10.

The principle
Finding the best defence does not necessarily mean holding on to the lead at all cost. Indeed, it often pays to make declarer do his own work by losing the lead deliberately, but without risk. In the above example it would be fatal for East to switch to a spade or a diamond. A passive defence, however, will leave South with a critical guess which, remembering the bidding, he will not find easy to resolve.

51. Game all; dealer South. Contract: 4H by South.

```
              ♠ K Q 4
              ♡ 10 9 4
              ◇ A K J 10 5
              ♣ 7 2
         ┌─────────┐      ♠ 9 8 6 4 2
         │    N    │      ♡ A 5 3
         │  W   E  │      ◇ 6
         │    S    │      ♣ A 8 6 4
         └─────────┘
```

The bidding

S	N
1♡	2◇
2♡	4♡

West leads the king of clubs. How should East plan the defence?

Masterminding the defence

51. Game all; dealer South.   Contract: 4H by South.

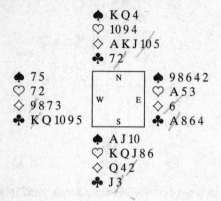

```
              ♠ K Q 4
              ♡ 10 9 4
              ◇ A K J 10 5
              ♣ 7 2
  ♠ 7 5          N          ♠ 9 8 6 4 2
  ♡ 7 2                     ♡ A 5 3
  ◇ 9 8 7 3    W   E        ◇ 6
  ♣ K Q 10 9 5    S         ♣ A 8 6 4
              ♠ A J 10
              ♡ K Q J 8 6
              ◇ Q 4 2
              ♣ J 3
```

The defence

Just as a declarer has to plan ahead, so must a defender. Unless East appreciates that he is in the enviable position of being able to mastermind the defence, declarer may well succeed. East should overtake the ♣K with the ♣A and return the ◇6. When trumps are played, East wins with the ace, puts his partner in with the ♣Q and scores a diamond ruff for the setting trick.

The principle

Sometimes a defender, who can 'see' exactly what is needed to defeat the contract, must conduct the defence virtually unaided. The principle is to think ahead before playing to the first trick and try to form a viable plan. On the above hand, if East does not recognize that he possesses the key to the defence, and supinely plays an encouraging club, the only chance of defeating the contract will be lost.

52. Game all; dealer South.   Contract: 4S by South.

                    ♠ 10975
                    ♡ A J 10 3
                    ◇ K 6 5
                    ♣ 6 4
    ♠ K 8   ┌─────────────┐
    ♡ K Q 5   │   N   │
    ◇ J 10 9 8   │ W   E │
    ♣ 10 8 5 3   │   S   │
                   └─────────────┘

The bidding

            S   N
            1♠   2♠
            4♠

West leads the knave of diamonds which is covered by dummy's
king and East's ace. East continues with the queen and another
diamond, ruffed by South. South now leads the six of hearts.
How should West plan the defence?

Second player plays high

52. Game all; dealer South.   Contract: 4S by South.

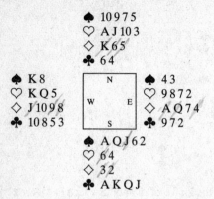

```
                    ♠ 10 9 7 5
                    ♡ A J 10 3
                    ♢ K 6 5
                    ♣ 6 4
     ♠ K 8                        ♠ 4 3
     ♡ K Q 5         N            ♡ 9 8 7 2
     ♢ J 10 9 8    W   E          ♢ A Q 7 4
     ♣ 10 8 5 3      S            ♣ 9 7 2
                    ♠ A Q J 6 2
                    ♡ 6 4
                    ♢ 3 2
                    ♣ A K Q J
```

The defence

West should contribute the ♡Q at trick four. With two tricks already in the bag, and the ♠K to come, West cannot afford to be mean with his high cards, nor must he play by 'rule' rather than thinking things out for himself ('Second hand plays low, third hand plays high', is an old adage from whist). If West does play the ♡5 on the first round there is a danger that South will put in the ♡10, losing no tricks in the suit at all.

The principle

There is a considerable difference between sacrificing high cards thoughtlessly and playing them to ensure a vital defensive trick. When you can see that if you play low declarer can hardly go wrong, you must play a high card. In the above hand, even if West does not hold the ♠K, it is still correct to play the ♡Q on the first round. Maybe East has another trick, in any case it cannot gain to duck.